The Jesup North Pacific Expedition

Edited by FRANZ BOAS

VOL. 1
PART VI

Includes INDEX

To VOL. 1: Parts I-VI

AMS PRESS
NEW YORK

The Jesup North Pacific Expedition

Edited by FRANZ BOAS

Memoir of the American Museum

of

Natural History

NEW YORK

VOL. I ⁻ PART VI

ARCHAEOLOGY

OF THE

THOMPSON RIVER REGION,

BRITISH COLUMBIA

BY

HARLAN INGERSOLL SMITH

NEW YORK, 1900

Library of Congress Cataloging in Publication Data

Smith, Harlan Ingersoll, 1872-1940.
    Archaeology of the Thompson River region, British Columbia.

    Reprint of the 1900 ed. published in New York, which was issued as v. 2
of Memoirs of the American Museum of Natural History, Anthropology, v. 1,
pt. 6, and as v. 1, pt. 6 of Publications of the Jesup North Pacific Expedition.
    1. Indians of North America—British Columbia—Antiquities. 2. British
Columbia—Antiquities. 3. Thompson Valley, B. C.—Antiquities. I. Title.
II. Series: American Museum of Natural History, New York. Memoirs ; v. 2.
III. Series: The Jesup North Pacific Expedition Publications; v. 1, pt. 6.
E78.B9S63   1975   971.1'41   73-3515
ISBN 0-404-58117-X

Reprinted from the edition of 1900, New York
First AMS edition published, 1975
Manufactured in the United States of America

International Standard Book Number:
Complete Set: 0-404-58100-5
Volume 1 pt. 6: 0-404-58117-X

AMS PRESS, INC.
New York, N.Y. 10003

LIST OF ILLUSTRATIONS.

PLATES.

VI. — ARCHÆOLOGY OF THE THOMPSON RIVER REGION, BRITISH COLUMBIA.

By HARLAN I. SMITH.

PLATES XXIV–XXVI.

In the following pages are contained the results of archæological investigations carried on by the writer for the Jesup North Pacific Expedition in the Thompson River region, between Spences Bridge and Kamloops. The archæology of Lytton, a town situated at the confluence of Thompson and Fraser Rivers, has been described in Part III of this volume. Further researches were carried on at Spences Bridge, Kamloops, and in Nicola Valley.[1]

Spences Bridge is situated on Thompson River, twenty-two miles above Lytton, and about one mile below the mouth of Nicola River. At this place Thompson River flows through a narrow valley, about eight hundred feet above sea-level, between steep mountains cut out by its tributaries from the rolling plateau which extends from the Coast Range to the western slope of the Gold Range. The climate is dry, and, except where irrigation is resorted to, vegetation is scanty; but open timber is found in the higher valleys. Cactus, sagebrush, greasewood, and bunch-grass grow on the slopes, and cottonwood-trees border the streams. Great numbers of salmon that ascend Thompson River turn up Nicola River.

Kamloops (Plate XXIV) is situated ninety-five miles above Lytton, at the confluence of North Thompson and South Thompson Rivers, in the central part of southern British Columbia. The river here flows through a comparatively wide bottom-land, at an altitude of eleven hundred and sixty feet. The surrounding country is a rolling plateau. The climate is as dry as at Lytton and Spences Bridge, so that vegetation is equally scanty and similar in character. The neighboring mountains have less timber than those near Lytton; and the open hillsides, which are covered with bunch-grass and greasewood, are favorable for grazing. The Kamloops Indians state that formerly great herds of elk inhabited these hills, and that the neighboring tribes, as well as they themselves, hunted them. Salmon were also used for food, although the number of fish that reach this point is not as great as the number that ascend to Spences Bridge or up Nicola River. Consequently roots and berries, as well as deer and bear, were probably more extensively used than at places farther down the stream. Just below Kamloops the Thompson widens into Kamloops Lake, where wild fowl and fish abound and are easily accessible. A rocky cliff on the north shore of the lake, near the

---

[1] See map, p. 166, Part IV.

mouth of Tranquille River, bears numerous pictographs painted in red. The cliff is locally known as "Battle Bluff."

A large burial-place and village-site on the Indian reserve, on a low sandy stretch immediately north of Kamloops bridge, has been known for some time, but no full account of it has been published. The whole point bounded by North Thompson and South Thompson Rivers, Pauls Creek, and the mountains to the northeast of these, has for a long time been used by Indians as a camping-ground. The modern Indian village is situated at the northwestern limit of this area, near North Thompson River. A slough extends east and west between the present village and the old burial-place. Specimens collected on this site are in the Museum of the Geological Survey of Canada, in the Provincial Museum at Victoria, B. C., and in private cabinets.

The valley of Nicola River in its lower part is deep and narrow, while in its upper part it passes through an open rolling country, similar in character to the plateau north and south of Kamloops. A number of small streams run into Nicola Lake, which is situated about thirty-five miles south of Kamloops. The lake is about two thousand feet above sea-level. From here the river runs west about twenty-two miles, then northwest about the same distance. There it reaches Thompson River at an altitude of about eight hundred feet. The whole river is therefore rapid and shallow. Formerly bear and elk were abundant on the plateau. Trout are plentiful in Nicola Lake and its tributaries. The Indians of this valley have commercial intercourse with Kamloops to the north, Lytton and Boston Bar to the west, Similkameen to the south, and with the Okanagon to the east.

There are numerous rock-slides (Plate XXV) along the base of some of the cliffs. The examination of graves reported by Indians to be in these slides was the main object of explorations in this valley.

In June, 1897, a series of explorations was made in the vicinity of Spences Bridge and Kamloops. In May, 1898, and in May, 1899, these sites were revisited. In October, 1899, an exploring trip was made in Nicola Valley from its mouth to the head of Nicola Lake. The following descriptions are based upon these explorations. The accompanying illustrations are from drawings by Mr. Rudolf Weber. The botanical specimens have been identified by Mr. Willard N. Clute of Bing-hamton, N. Y. The writer also wishes to acknowledge his indebtedness to Rev. Father J. M. Le Jeune of Kamloops, to Mr. James Teit of Spences Bridge, and to the chiefs of the Indian bands visited, all of whom rendered valuable assistance in carrying on his field-work.

At Spences Bridge a single grave was the most interesting site explored. It was located on the edge of the first terrace overlooking Thompson River from the north, on the Murray Ranch, about a quarter of a mile above the ferry. There are numerous old graves near by, on an island near the north bank of Thompson River, which the Indians did not wish us to explore, while they assisted in exploring the first grave, which had been unknown to them. This grave contained no evidence of contact with whites. On the other hand, there is no positive evidence pointing to great antiquity.   Fabrics that were buried with the body, and wooden poles in the surrounding soil, were still in a fair state of preservation.   A detailed description of this grave will be found on p. 434.

Single graves and little burial-grounds of greater or less antiquity are found at frequent intervals, often less than a mile apart.   Several single graves are on the hillside above the burial mentioned before.   A small cemetery is situated on the south side of the river, not far below the mouth of Nicola River; a second one is just below the settlement on the south side of the river; a third one is on the opposite side; and a fourth one is about half a mile farther down, also on the north side of the valley.   One burial-ground below the Indian village was covered by a gravel-slide which was caused by the encroachment of the river upon the deep gravel-beds which fill the valley.

About four miles above Spences Bridge, on the north side of the valley, are several pits surrounded by embankments, which mark the sites of ancient underground houses.   Excavations in these pits resulted in finding broken bones of deer, bear, salmon, etc., charcoal, burned and crackled stones, and other evidences of occupancy.   Similar pits are located on the same side of the valley just above the settlement, and on the south side near the mouth of Nicola River.   Between this place and the railroad-station at Spences Bridge the river has cut into the bank, and exposed several old burials.   Here are also remains of underground houses.   More of them may be seen near the Indian village just below the railroad-station, and a large number are located on the low terrace close to the south bank of the river, about a mile down the valley.   Excavations in these show that the fireplace was near the centre of the house.   Numerous broken bones of food-animals were found with ashes and charcoal.   Several skin-scrapers made of stone were found on the surface of the circular embankments (see Fig. 355).   Small pits of similar appearance, but deeper in proportion to their diameter, are found near these house-sites, and are supposed to be remains of caches or cellars.   Chipped points of glassy basalt for arrows, spears, etc., chipped skin-scrapers made of stone, stone hammers or pestles, and bowlders bearing paintings in red,[1] are frequently found on the surface near Spences Bridge.

At Kamloops attention was directed particularly to the large burial-ground and camp-site already described.   Except where held in place by an occasional sagebrush, the light yellowish gray sand is ever shifting over this site, so that the depth of the remains varies daily, and the original order of burial has been much disturbed.   Burned and crackled bowlders hold in place conical piles of sand from twenty to thirty feet in diameter.   These are evidently the places where stones have been heated to be used in cooking roots or for boiling food in baskets. Strewn over the entire site are found the bones of food-animals, stray bones from graves, burned and crackled firestones, and other objects, such as dentalium shells, copper beads, and flat oblong beads made of bone.   The last named were usually found in little patches near traces of fires, and were frequently charred.

---

[1] See Part IV, Plate XIX.

Chipped points for knives, arrows, etc., wedges made of antler, and stone pestles or hammers, were also discovered.

At intervals along the river-bank, from the western limit of this site to the Government Indian School, about two miles to the east, are remains of underground houses, which are most numerous near the school. They vary from about fifteen to thirty feet in diameter, and close to them are traces of cache-pits five or six feet in diameter. There are also remains of underground houses at the south end of the bridge. In one of these a number of willow-trees six to eight inches in diameter are growing.

The "Government Site" is located north of the slough, on a flat at the base of the foot-hills close to the school. Here the shifting sand has exposed the remains of cremated children, together with dentalium shells, flat oblong bone beads, and chipped cache forms of glassy basalt.

The "Government Hill Site" is located on the brow of the foot-hills leading to the mountains, about a hundred feet above the flat northwest of the school, and northeast of the large burial-ground. Here water may have been obtained from the slough at the base of the hills. At this site also the wind constantly shifts the dry sand, and the surface is strewn with material similar to that on the large burial-ground. Burials found here were not claimed by the present Indians as belonging to their ancestors, although an iron awl with bone handle (see Fig. 357*d*) was found. Sagebrush fabrics and wood were also found in the graves, but these would naturally last for a long time in the dry sand.

In one of the ravines cutting the foot-hills were quantities of angular pieces of rock, which seem to be of the same material as that of which the chipped implements found in this region were made. It was not determined whether an outcrop of this rock was uncovered by erosion of the ravine, or whether these angular pieces had been carried down by water from a point higher up the hillside. Following up the ravine, their occurrence became less frequent, and finally they seemed to be entirely absent. Workshops were not discovered in this ravine, but at several places on the Government Hill Site chips of glassy basalt were found in caches uncovered by the wind, and accompanied in one instance by small pebbles possibly used as chipping-hammers, and fragments of bone that may have been used in flaking. Cache forms and finished implements were found in the vicinity. On the whole, these places seem to have been small workshops.

The first whites to reach this vicinity were the Hudson Bay Company's agents, who built a block-house on the point west of the mouth of North Thompson River. Here were found the graves of the Indians who first met the whites. The bodies were buried stretched out on the back, with heads west, in wooden coffins put together with blacksmith-made iron nails. Near these graves were traces of underground houses. The Indians raised no objections to the exploration of these graves, although they knew that they were those of their immediate ancestors. They did not know to what people the graves at the other sites at Kamloops belonged.

About two miles below this point, on the northern side of the river, is a wind-swept sand-knoll where evidences of a village-site were found. Near the mouth of Tranquille River, on the north side of Kamloops Lake, above the red paintings on Battle Bluff, were evidences of still another village-site.

In Nicola Valley, at lĭkᴸa'qᴇtᴇn, about nine miles above the mouth and on the east side of the river, were a number of graves (Plate XXV, Fig. 1). The bodies had been placed upon the surface at the foot of a rock-slide or talus slope, and were covered by disturbing the slope sufficiently to cause rocks to slide down over them.[1] These graves are usually marked by a few rocks piled up on them ; but the pile is so low, that it is difficult to distinguish it from other parts of the talus slope. In some cases a branch was inserted among the rocks over the grave, and extended down to the body. One skeleton, resting upon the rock-slide, was in a little tent of poles covered with mats made of the stalks of the common cat-tail (*Typha latifolia* L.). The rock-slide had been worked down around the tent to a height of about two feet over the skeleton. There were no objects found with the body or in the tent. Another grave was without a tent, but contained a celt and chipped basalt points. The Indians knew of these graves, and considered them as belonging to the Thompson Indians, although they did not care much for them. Numerous pits, the remains of underground houses and food-caches, were located on the flat between this slide and the river.

At a point four miles farther up the valley, or thirteen miles from its mouth, is a rocky bluff which the Indians call Ka'iatamus a canᴇx, or " the shooting rock," on account of the following custom : The young men, when passing along the trail between the river and the rock, used to try their skill at lodging an arrow on its top. At the southern base of this cliff is a talus slope in which are a number of burials marked by posts and twigs. One of the posts is carved at the top to repre-sent a human face. These graves are also known by the Indians to be those of the Thompsons, but they care very little for them, because no near relatives of the people buried there are living. There are house-pits about a mile below this place, also about a quarter of a mile above it, and at various camping-places throughout the valley. They are so numerous that notes of all the sites were not taken. At some of them are cache-pits, and also circular saucer-shaped depressions which mark sites of summer lodges. The former are deep, and surrounded by embankments.

The graves of two children and one man, the latter known to have been buried in the fifties, were explored on the terrace overlooking Nicola River from the south, at the mouth of Nicola Lake and due south of the bridge. These graves were about eighteen inches deep, and above each of them was a pile of five or six bowlders. Red pictographs were reported by the Indians to be on a rocky promontory which we saw near the middle of the lake, on its northern shore.

At Nxaxtetᴇx·, near Qê''ɪamix, on the Indian reserve at the eastern limit of Nicola Lake, south of Nicola River and of the church on the reserve, is an outcrop of rock in the Meander Hills. This is about three miles north of Quilchena

---

[1] See Part IV, p. 330.

(Qwiltca'na).   There are three main talus slopes between this knoll and the lake, in all of which were graves marked by sticks and twigs.   Charlie Tcilaxitca, who is about sixty years of age and a brother of the chief of this reserve, related that when he first saw the place, it resembled a patch of small dead trees, so numerous were the twigs marking graves on the slope.   The rocks were piled up over the graves, but the piles were so low that they were difficult to find, except when marked by twigs (Plate XXV, Fig. 2).

Ulula'mqĕn, or Iron-Head, a man about seventy years of age, who was born at the lower end of Nicola Lake, and lived on this reserve, gave the following history of these graves.   One spring, when his father was a young man, and before he himself was born, about fifty Nicola Athapascans were living in an underground house where the church is now.[1]   From there on to the flat close to the lake, between it and the rock-slides, a party of about a hundred Thompson Indians were camping in lodges among the bushes which skirt the shore, and give the place its name.   A few of them had come from near Spences Bridge, and many from Lytton, to fish in Nicola Lake.   In the evening one of the Nicola Athapascans noticed some people without horses walking along the hillsides on the northern border of the lake.   He reported what he had seen, but the people thought they were only hunters or some persons out for a stroll.   All went well until some time after dark, when they heard a cry like that of an owl from the hill-side to the eastward.   Then a coyote-cry answered, and so on, along the hillside surrounding the camp on the eastward, until the cries of two owls, one fox, two coyotes, and a bald-headed eagle, had been heard.   The fires were burning brightly in the dark night, and the people were all eating.   When they noticed these cries, they grew suspicious, especially when later they heard the note of a robin nearer the camp than that bird would naturally come.   A boy was sent out to see who uttered the cry.   He objected; but the people made him go, never thinking it might be an enemy's cry.   Being afraid, the boy stuck a lighted piece of pitch-wood in his head-dress.   When he had gone a little distance, a Shuswap warrior, one of a party from near Kamloops, who had probably made the noise, jumped up and struck him on the head, killing him.   Immediately, while most of the people were still eating, not having had time to learn of this murder, the war-cries of the entire attacking party were heard.   The enemy consisted of about two hundred young warriors.   They killed the whole fishing-party except a few young women, whom they made their slaves.   Two Thompsons, one man and one woman, escaped by swimming across the lake.   All the people in the underground house were killed.   The narrator did not know of any noted Indians being present among the victims.   The Shuswap left most of the property of the slain behind, in their haste to return before an avenging party could be organized.

Shortly after this, Nkwala', a chief of the Nicola Athapascans, but partly of Okanagon blood, arrived with a party of friends from his home on the eastern side of Douglas Lake.   He was one of the greatest chiefs of the whole region,

---

[1] Remains of underground houses were found where he said, and were probably known to him.

and for him Nicola Valley is named.   He was greatly surprised to learn of the massacre, and pained to see the dead that had been left by the Shuswap warriors. Some of the children had been tied in pairs, and thrown over the handles of spears that had been stuck into the house-poles ; and a number of the older persons, as well as some of the children, had been disembowelled.   He set out to bury these people hastily, which took his party over a day and a half.   No avenging party was sent by the Nicola Athapascans.   The Thompsons sent out a party, which went to Kamloops by way of Douglas Lake, and returned by the Thompson River trails.   Their success is unknown.   The old men told the narrator that all of the dogs were killed and buried with their owners, so far as these were known ; but those whose masters were not known were killed and buried separately.   A large number of dentalium shells were buried with one body.   Stone axes, kettles (one of which was of copper), and other things, were also buried with their owners when known.   A double-bladed iron knife, probably secured by trade from the United States, was buried with one body.   The people had no guns at that time ; and such horses as they had, if any, were taken possession of by relatives.   The Thompsons and Athapascans, being close friends, were buried together indiscriminately.   Iron-Head had never heard that any burials were made in the rock-slide before or since this massacre.   The chief, however, said that later on, an Indian who had died of small-pox had been buried there, it being an out-of-the-way place.

Resources.—The resources of the prehistoric people of the Thompson River region, as indicated by the results of these explorations, were practically the same as those found at Lytton.[1]   According to Dawson,[2] fine-grained augite-porphyrite, or basalt, is abundant in the Arrow-stone Hills and near the head of Cache Creek, a tributary of Bonaparte River, which empties into the Thompson from the north, between Kamloops and Spences Bridge.   Although objects made of this material are found in the Lillooet Valley, and even in the Fraser Delta, yet it seems to have been more frequently used for chipped implements the nearer the Thompson River region is approached.   One drill-point made of andesitic lava was found, and also one object made of aragonite.   Green stones[3] are perhaps as numerous among the bowlders near Spences Bridge as they are at Lytton.   Bowlders of nephrite (identified by Mr. George F. Kunz) resembling the same material from Lytton and the Thompson River region were found by the writer on the beach at the mouth of Nootsack River, in the State of Washington.   Flat pebbles of the same material, sharpened and partly cut into strips to form celts, were also

[1] See Part III, pp. 132, ff.

[2] Notes on the Shuswap People of British Columbia (Transactions of the Royal Society of Canada, Section II, 1891, p. 35) ; also American Anthropologist, N.S., Vol. I, October, 1899, p. 766.

[3] See Part III, p. 132 ; Notes on the Shuswap People of British Columbia, by George M. Dawson (Trans. Roy. Soc. Canada, Section II, 1891, pp. 11, 18) ; Note on the Occurrence of Jade in British Columbia, and its Employment by the Natives, by George M. Dawson (Canadian Record of Science, Vol. II, No. 6, April, 1887, p. 364) ; Notes on Specimens of Nephrite from British Columbia, by B. J. Harrington (Trans. Roy. Soc. Canada, Section III, 1890, p. 61) ; and other papers referred to in these publications.

found. It seems that these bowlders are widely distributed, and that wherever they occurred they were used for making implements.

Here as elsewhere tough rocks, such as diorites, were employed for hammers, pestles, etc. Yellow ochre, of a more reddish color than that seen at Lytton,[1] was found at Kamloops, while white calcareous or infusorial earths were not found in this region, although there is no proof that they were not used. Fragments of rock bearing galena were found at Kamloops, as was also an iron awl.

Some points (Fig. 336) suitable for arrows were made of bone. Beaver-teeth were made into dice. Bone of the whale (identified by Prof. H. F. Osborn) was imported from the seacoast, and made into war-clubs of a form typical of this region. It is possible that it was imported over the same route as were the dentalium shells, which until recently came through the Chilcotin country, from the region north of Vancouver Island. This is further emphasized by the absence of clubs of this material along Lower Fraser River.

Pecten shells were found, but no olivella-shell objects were seen above Lytton. Shells of the fresh-water unio were found in little patches about three feet in diameter at the four largest sites at Kamloops in sufficient numbers to indicate that this animal was used for food.

Fragments of matting made of cat-tail stalks, fabrics of sagebrush-bark, fibre of cedar, and charred bearberries, were found in the graves, but seeds of *Lythospermum* were not seen.

Hunting and Fishing; Digging Roots. — The implements used in procuring food in this region were fully as numerous as at Lytton, and of a similar character. The chipped points for arrows, spears, knives, etc., were usually made of glassy

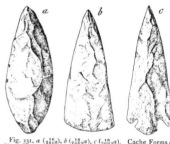

Fig. 331, *a* ($2\frac{16}{100}$), *b* ($2\frac{18}{109}a$), *c* ($\frac{16}{2093}a$). Cache Forms of Glassy Basalt. Kamloops. ½ nat. size.

basalt. Numerous caches containing chips and blades of this material were found. Blades of the forms shown in Fig. 331 were abundant. The chips and flakes which were found in lots of thirty to a hundred in the caches are rather large, curved to the natural fracture, and often show bulbs of percussion. They are similar to chips and flakes from other regions. Some show secondary chipping along one or more edges. Although usually waste material from the manufacture of chipped implements, they were undoubtedly sometimes used, here as elsewhere, for cutting.

Points chipped from this material are very numerous, and exhibit a great variety of forms. A typical series is illustrated in Fig. 332. One of these points (Fig. 332, *c*) was found crushed into pieces of wood resembling parts of a bow, so that it seemed to be hafted in the wood. The specimen shown in Fig. 332 *f* is slightly polished, and its edges are rounded, probably by the sand blowing against it. Fig. 332, *i, j,* shows typical points much like the usual forms, save that each

[1] See Part III, p. 133.

of these is specialized by serrations on one side.   Typical forms made of other materials are shown in Fig. 333.   Some of these are made of white chalcedony (Fig. 333, *a* and *c*), another one of waxy yellow chalcedony (Fig. 333, *b*), and a fourth one of chert (Fig. 333, *d*).

Four beautifully chipped complex forms of glassy basalt are shown in Fig. 334, *b* to *e*. The form shown in Fig. 334 *a* was collected

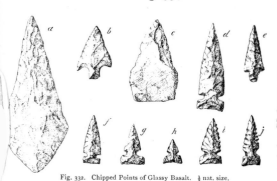

Fig. 332. Chipped Points of Glassy Basalt. ½ nat. size.

a (₂⁵₅₈), *b* (₇⁵₅₂*a*), *c* (₂⁵₅₇*a*), *d* (₂⁵₄₈*a*), *f* (₂⁵₇₅), *g* (₂⁵₅₉), *i* (₂⁵₅₉*a*), *j* (₂⁵₅₉*b*), Kamloops; *e* (₂⁵₇₇), *h* (₂⁵₅₉*a*), Spences Bridge.

by Mr. Teit from a cache of badly formed points found near Spences Bridge.   The Indians maintained that it was a piece of arrow-stone shaped by the Raven for no particular purpose, that the Raven shaped the arrow-stone according to his fancy, but that most of the forms he made resemble arrow-heads.   Possibly these may have been used for scarifying the body or for surgical operations.

Fig. 333. *a* (₂⁵₅₉), *b* (₂⁵₅₇), *c* (₂⁵₅₉), *d* (₈⁵₅₉*a*). Chipped Points made of Chalcedony and Chert. Kamloops. ¼ nat. size.

Two points rubbed out of slate have been found in this region (Fig. 335).
These, like the sea-shells and bone of the whale, probably came from the coast, where such forms are common, or they are at least imitations of forms originally belonging to the coast.

Points for arrow and spear heads rubbed out of bone (Fig. 336) were not uncommon.   Although I did not find any at Lytton, it is safe to assume that they were used there as well.   The base of the specimen shown in Fig. 336 *b* is thin and sufficiently wedge-shaped to be readily inserted in an arrow-shaft, while

Fig. 334.   Fig. 335.

Fig. 334. Complex Chipped Points of Glassy Basalt. *a* (₁⁵₅₈), Spences Bridge; *b* (₇⁵₃₃*c*), *c* (₇⁵₅₃ *b*), *d* (₁⁵₅₃c), *e* (₇⁵₅₃*a*), Nicola Lake. ½ nat. size.

Fig. 335. Rubbed Points made of Slate. *a* (₂⁵₅₈), Kamloops; *b* (₄⁵₅₇*a*), Spences Bridge. ½ nat. size.

the specimen shown in Fig. 336 c has a base nearly cylindrical in form. In the charcoal and soil adhering to the specimen is the impression of primary wing-feathers, with the tips pointing towards its base. The specimen shown in Fig. 336 d is made of the heavy leg-bone of the elk or a like animal, and bears an artificial median groove on the surface opposite the marrow-canal. Of seven bone points that were buried with it, apparently in a pouch at the side of a body, three were of the form shown in Fig. 336 f, one of the form shown in Fig. 336 g, and two of the form shown in Fig. 336 h. Another one was apparently merely a splint with rounded back and hollowed front. Possibly two pieces like that shown in Fig. 336 f were placed one on each side of the one shown in Fig. 336 g, and lashed there by windings, to form the well-known salmon harpoon-head.[1] Each specimen of the shape shown in Fig. 336 f is considerably decomposed for about half its length from the tapering end, while the less acute end is better preserved. The different states of preservation of the two ends suggest that the points were inserted in a handle or held by windings, which affected the decomposition of the bone. The splint may have been simply a brace or filling between or outside of the others.   Possibly the other specimens were additional barbs.   This is not unlikely, because it is known that four-pronged spears were used by the Indians.   On the other hand, these specimens may have been used as the barbs of fish-

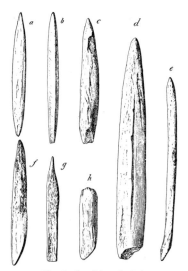

Fig. 336. Bone Points. ½ nat. size.
a ($_{2}\frac{4}{6}a$), b ($_{2}\frac{4}{6}b$), d, f-h ($_{2}\frac{4}{6}$ a, b, c, d), Kamloops ;
c ($_{2}\frac{1}{6}\frac{8}{3}$), e ($_{2}\frac{1}{6}\frac{8}{1}a$), Spences Bridge.

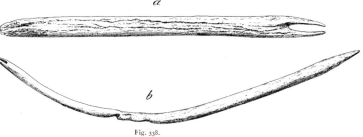

Fig. 337. Fig. 338.
Fig. 337, a ($_{6}\frac{4}{6}\frac{9}{2}$), b ($_{2}\frac{1}{6}\frac{9}{1}$) c ($_{2}\frac{1}{6}\frac{0}{9}a$). Harpoon-points made of Bone. Kamloops. ½ nat. size.
Fig. 338, a ($_{2}\frac{1}{6}\frac{9}{3}$), Bone object, Kamloops ; b ($_{2}\frac{1}{6}\frac{9}{3}$), Wooden object, Spences Bridge. ½ nat. size.

spears.[2]   Fig. 336 e illustrates one of seven specimens, all of similar form but varying in size, found in the pouch at the side of a grave explored at Spences

[1] See Part IV, Fig. 231.   [2] Ibid., Fig. 232.

Bridge. Two of the specimens of this lot show well-preserved impressions of winding, exactly as would be the case if they formed parts of a harpoon-point.[1]

A bone harpoon-point made wholly of one piece of material, and with a barb, was found (Fig. 337, *a*). The barb, however, is broken off. The base is wedge-shaped, and could easily be inserted in the split end of a handle. Such harpoon-points, I was told by Baptiste, an old shaman who is still familiar with the ancient implements of the Indians, were used for spearing beaver.[2] A similar point, also said to be used for beaver-spearing, was secured by Mr. Teit from the Indians at Spences Bridge. Two other harpoon-points (Fig. 337, *b, c*) are much burned, and, as both are broken, their original shape cannot be determined. There are many pieces still less perfect, which were found scattered on the surface of the large burial-ground at Kamloops, while other pieces were found with cremated bones of children at the Government Site.

Fig. 338 *a* illustrates a bone object found on the surface of the Government Hill at Kamloops. It has been bleached and somewhat warped by the sun. The notch in the end extends slightly down the sides, but shows no rubbing.

Fig. 338 *b* illustrates a similar-shaped speci-men made of wood, which was found in a woven pouch in the grave at Spences Bridge. Still adhering to it are shreds of cedar-bark, while traces of red ochre cover it. The notch is rectangular, and the other end of the specimen is pointed like a sharpened lead-pencil. These specimens seem to be fore-shafts for arrows or spears,— the former possibly for a spear, while the latter, being delicate, would be more appropriate for a small arrow.

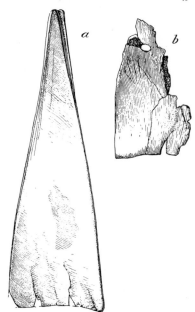

In a grave near Nicola Lake were found fragments of a wooden bow of lenticular cross-section ornamented with parallel, irreg-ularly arranged, cuneiform incisions.[3] Pieces of wood, some of which may have been part of a bow, were found in a grave at the mouth of Nicola Lake, and pieces of wood found in the second grave on the Govern-ment Hill at Kamloops resemble a bow of the type shown in Fig. 220, Part IV.

Fig. 339, *a* (₄₅₅ₐ), *b* (₄₅₅ₐ). Sap-scrapers. Kamloops. ½ nat. size.

Digging-sticks were used in the region, several of the handles made of antler having been found. Many of them are deco-rated by incised designs.[4]

---

[1] See Part IV, Fig. 231.   [2] See Part III, Fig. 20, which shows a specimen probably used for the same purpose.
[3] See Part IV, Fig. 216.   [4] See Part III, p. 137 ; Part IV, p. 231.

For securing soft inner bark or sap for food, the Indians use bone scrapers, with which the trunk of the tree is scraped after the outer bark has been removed.[1] The specimens shown in Fig. 339 probably served the same purpose. One of these (Fig. 339, a) is made from the shoulder-blade of some large mammal. It is consequently very thin. The edges show that the bone was cut by grooving or incising each side, and breaking, in the same manner as the pieces of serpentine and nephrite were detached from bowlders. The broken edges were then smoothed by rubbing, and the short side was sharpened. A second specimen is also made of bone. It is slightly thicker than the other. It shows no marks of cutting, and has sharp edges on all sides. A third one (Fig. 339, b) is smaller, but similar to the first. It is perforated, possibly for suspension, and does not show marks of cutting along its edges.[2]

In Fig. 340 a is shown a bone implement made from a fragment of a long bone, slightly worked at the base, and shaped like a paper-cutter at the point. Fig.

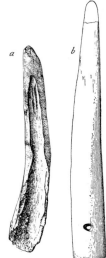

340 b represents another bone implement, very thin, with rounded edges at the base, and is shaped like the former. It is perforated at the centre, about an inch from the base, the hole having been drilled or scraped from both sides. These two implements may have been used for cutting inner bark when the sap runs in April.[3]

Tubes about four inches long, made from bird-bones cut off squarely at the ends, were secured. These were probably used for drinking.[4]

Pieces of birch-bark with perforations resembling small needle-holes were found; and in the second grave on the Government Hill a little dish was secured. It was made by turning up the sides of a piece of birch-bark, folding in the ends, and stitching them with a piece of bark. The specimen may have been a drinking-cup, similar to those in use up to recent times. The present Indians make such dishes in which to market wild strawberries.

Preparation of Food. — Stone pestles served for crush-

Fig. 340, *a* (₂⁰⁰₀₃), *b* (₂¹⁰₈₀).
Bone Implements. Kamloops. ½
nat. size.

ing dried meat, berries, etc., as well as for driving wedges, splitting wood, and in like industries. Many of these pestles are mere cylinders of tough rock, often but slightly changed from the natural pebble by a little pecking or rubbing. One of those found is over a foot in length. The typical form, which is common to this region, and to the upper Columbia near Spokane, however, has a conoid body with a rounded or hat-shaped top (Fig. 341, *a*, *b*). In some cases the top is of the form of a face or

---

[1] See Part IV, p. 233.
[2] See Part III, Fig. 95, which was probably also used as a sap-scraper ; not as a pendant, as stated on p. 151.
[3] Ibid, Fig. 51, which figure was believed by Michel of Lytton to represent such an implement.
[4] See Part IV, p. 313.

animal head (Fig. 341, *c*; see also Fig. 295, Part IV). The last-named specimen has a cylindrical striking-head, which resembles that of the typical pestles of Lytton. It might easily have been brought from there; and it is surprising that no more pestles with cylindrical striking-heads have been imported into this region.

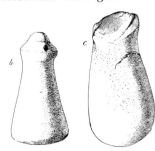

Fig. 341. Stone Hammers. ¼ nat. size.

a ($\frac{216}{240}$), *b* ($\frac{240}{237}$), Kamloops; *c* ($\frac{210}{240}$), Spences Bridge.

Flat oval bowlders, like those seen at Lytton, are frequently found scattered on the surface of the sites. The typical specimen is made of granite, and shows a decided saucer-shaped depression in the centre of one side. This tends to confirm the belief that these objects were used as anvils upon which to crush food or pound other material. Baptiste said that small stones were used as anvils upon which to crush food in mouthful quantities for rich, toothless old persons when travelling. He said that these persons would use a large stone when at home, but that a small one was lighter to carry when travelling. The food was placed between two pieces of skin and crushed with a small pestle. Large flat pieces of sandstone, on which food was rubbed,[1] were not found in this region.

The large stone mortar shown in Fig. 342 was found cached as described on p. 436. It is made of granite, with bottom slightly concave. The bowl is about six inches across by four inches deep, and fairly smooth.[2] The little stone mortar shown in Fig. 343 has a rather smooth, saucer-shaped bowl, with a smaller pecked pit in the base. Around it outside are four incised lines that are somewhat effaced, the specimen apparently having been last used as a hammer-stone. Mortars of the type shown in Fig. 342

Fig. 342.   Fig. 343.

Fig. 342 ($\frac{114}{200}$). Stone Mortar. Kamloops. ¼ nat. size.

Fig. 343 ($\frac{10}{230}$). Stone Mortar. Kamloops. ½ nat. size.

---

[1] See Part III, p. 139.

[2] According to information secured by Professor Boas some years ago, while at Kamloops, a large stone dish, made of serpentine or steatite, was found there in 1874, and is said to have been sent to Geneva, Switzerland; another was said to have been secured by Professor Haliburton and sent to Ottawa; while a third and fourth were taken to Victoria by Judge O'Riley and Dr. Ash. The last-named specimen is said to have represented a woman in a sitting posture, with a snake sculptured on her back, where was also a cup-shaped depression.

were not found west of Kamloops.   They are common, however, to the south, in Columbia Valley and in California.

Fish-knives made of slate, like those found at Lytton, were rare at Kamloops.   They were not found at Spences Bridge or in Nicola Valley.   The scarcity of slate knives among the finds is probably due to chance or to the fact that dried fish was a comparatively unimportant article of diet.   It cannot be due to lack of contact with Coast tribes, because other objects are found, made of material imported from the coast, or exhibiting in their form the influence of coast culture.   The slate knife illustrated in Fig. 344, like another one, has very dull edges, all of which are about equally rubbed or rounded, as would be the case had the object been used as a skin scraper.   There is a wide shallow groove, perhaps one-fourth the width of the specimen, running lengthwise near one edge, and on the other side a similar groove near the opposite edge.   These grooves disappear before reaching the ends of the specimen.

Fig. 344 ($\frac{16}{20}$). Fish-knife. Kamloops. ½ nat. size.

No shell spoons were found.   The conical piles of sand held in place by burned and crackled pebbles, that are described on p. 403, are undoubtedly the sites where roots were baked, after being covered with leaves and ashes.   The Indians boiled their food in baskets until recently.   The scattered burned and crackled stones, and the entire absence of pottery, suggest that it was the custom in the past.   We may naturally suppose that roasting before open fires was also as customary as it is now.

Habitations. — Here, as at Lytton, the ancient houses were similar to the underground houses inhabited by the Indians until within the last decade.[1]   This is proved by the numerous pits, each surrounded by a circular embankment, found at all of the sites visited (Part III, Plate XIII, Fig. 2, also pp. 403 ff).   Near them are often found the pits indicating ancient food-caches or cellars.

Tools. — Wedges made of elk-antler were of the same sort, and were as numerous in the graves and on the surface as at Lytton.   Undoubtedly they were here used for the same purposes, for splitting timbers, cutting firewood, and for general carpentry-work.   Some of these wedges are much battered by long use.   The one illustrated in Fig. 345 shows grooves at the sides similar to those which are seen on some of the stone celts, the antler having been partly cut through from both sides, and then broken before the wedge was rubbed to a point.   Some of the wedges were made of very small prongs of antler sharpened from both sides, and are almost small enough to serve as awls.

Fig. 345 ($\frac{16}{20}$).   Wedge made of Antler. Kamloops. ½ nat. size.

[1] See Part IV, pp. 192–195.

While the stone hammers or pestles with convex bases were possibly largely used for crushing food and for a variety of other purposes, yet those with concave bases were undoubtedly oftener used as hammers for driving wedges, etc.   The deeply-pitted hammer-stone, such as is found in the Great Lake region, was not seen, but tough pebbles were used for pounding.   Some of these are small, and battered on only one end.   Similar unbattered pebbles found with pieces of glassy basalt in the caches suggest that the former might have been chipping-hammers.   Others are mere pebbles the ends of which were flattened by use in pounding.   One of these hammers (Fig. 346) is very smooth on one side, while the opposite side is slightly polished.   The flattened ends are not battered, but appear as if the object had been used to pound some soft material, or as if while in use it had been protected, perhaps by being covered with skin.   It may have served as a club-head.[1]   The rubbed sides would tend to confirm the idea that it had been hafted.

The specimen shown in Fig. 347 is a pebble which has been notched or grooved on two edges.   It does not show any battered ends; but another object of the same kind is slightly abraded on one side.   These may have been sinkers for nets used when fishing in Kamloops Lake, or club-heads which were covered with skin when in use.   Round stones somewhat similar to these were covered with skin and used as balls.[2] Possibly some stones of the kind here described[3] may have been used for this purpose.

Stone celts, the longest specimens of which Baptiste

Fig. 346.

Fig. 347.

Figs. 346 (2⅜⅜), 347 (2¹⁰⁄₄₆).   Stone Hammers.   Kamloops.   ¼ nat. size.

Fig. 348 (2⅒₁).   Handle made of Antler.   Kamloops.   ½ nat. size.

said may have been used either as battle-axes or chisels,[4] were found throughout the entire region.

The bleached piece of antler shown in Fig. 348 was possibly the handle of a stone chisel.   The lower end is cut squarely across, and the upper end is bevelled. The specimen was found in pieces, the soft inner part of the antler being too much decomposed to determine whether the object was a handle or merely a cylinder of antler.   It is the only archæological evidence secured in this region that tends to prove a statement of Baptiste, that celt handles were made of antler.

The material of the celts is green stone, apparently such as was used for the

---

[1] See Part IV, Fig. 248.   [2] Ibid., p. 279.   [3] See Part III, p. 142.   [4] See Part IV, p. 183.

same purpose at Lytton. Those figured were identified as nephrite by Mr. George F. Kunz.

These celts vary in size. The largest one found measured nearly fourteen inches in length (Fig. 349, *a*), and the smallest barely two inches in length (Fig. 350, *b*). Both of these specimens are double-bladed, and, like nearly all celts of the region, show traces of the grooves by which they were cut out.[1]

Michel of Lytton stated that the horsetail rush (*Equisetum*) was used to start the grooves when cutting out pieces of nephrite.[2] After that, sharpened beaver-teeth, and finally quartz, sandstone, or nephrite, either with or without sand, was used. Mr. Teit refers to the use of the same plant for polishing.[3]

I have stated already[1] that various methods were used for cutting nephrite, and that the numerous fragments of sandstone showing bevelled or rounded edges, which were found at Lytton, were probably extensively used for this purpose. It would seem that those with rounded edges had been worn down in the process of cutting.

Fig. 349, *a* (₇₀³₀₀), *b* (₇₀⁵⁷₀₄), *c* (₇₀⁵⁹₀₉).   Celts made of Nephrite. East End Nicola Lake. ⅓ nat. size.

---

[1] See Part III, p. 143.

[2] See Part III, Fig. 49.   Michel probably meant steatite, of which pipes were made, and in cutting which beaver-teeth might have been used.

[3] See Part IV, p. 184.

Some pieces of slate with rubbed edges, found at Kamloops, may have served the same purpose; but pieces of sandstone similar to those found at Lytton were entirely absent. It may be that nephrite implements were not manufactured at any of the places investigated, as is also suggested by the scarcity of cut bowlders, of which a single specimen only was found; and this would account for the absence of these sandstone cutters. Some of the grooved bowlders found at Lytton have small artificial scratches on them, resembling glacial striæ, such as would be made by a few large grains of sand under a rubbing-stone.

The specimens shown in Fig. 349, a and b, have either been battered at one end and afterwards rubbed smooth purposely or by continued use, or one end had never been fully sharpened, leaving part of the fractured surface unpolished, while the edge itself was much rubbed. The specimen shown in Fig. 349 c has been cut across at its upper end by a groove on each side. The end was broken off at that point, and part of the fractured surface was rubbed smooth. The implement with slanting edge, shown in Fig. 350 a, might well have served for a knife, even without hafting. Some specimens were much worn by use, handling, or by sand being blown against them. Several have one side convex, the other flat.

Fig. 350, a (₈₁₃₈), b (₇₈₅₃). Celts made of Nephrite. Kamloops. ½ nat. size.

A few fragments of siliceous sandstone rubbed on the flat sides were found, which probably served as rough whetstones and for grinding implements into shape.

Whetstones, some of them similar to those found at Lytton, were frequently obtained on the surface and in graves. Sometimes several were found in a single grave. One of these (Fig. 351, a) is flat, and a groove runs diagonally across it, as if it had been used to sharpen a chisel-like object. Another one (Fig. 351, b) has also deep scratches. It is nearly square in cross-section. Still another one (Fig. 351, c) is of fine-grained schist rubbed on the edge, somewhat as are the gritstones used for cutting serpentine and nephrite; but it is concave in places, as if rubbed upon rather than used in ploughing a groove. Many of these whetstones were simple, finger-shaped pieces of slate or fine-grained schist rubbed on all sides.

Fig. 351. Whetstones. ½ nat. size.

a (₂₅₁₃₃a), b (₂₄₅₇), Kamloops; c (₇₆₄₅), Nicola Valley.

The frequent presence of beaver-teeth, not made into dice, in the caches and graves, although they were not cut, as were some found at Lytton,[1] suggests that

---

[1] See Part III, Fig. 49.

they were used for cutting or for chipping implements.   A piece of wood resembling a bow, into which was pressed a chipped stone point (Fig. 332, *c*), is the only object found which is suggestive of a knife-handle.

One bar of antler about a quarter of an inch in thickness and an inch wide, tapering to a narrow square end which was rubbed smooth, may have been used for chipping arrow-points, plaiting baskets, or for similar purposes.   According to

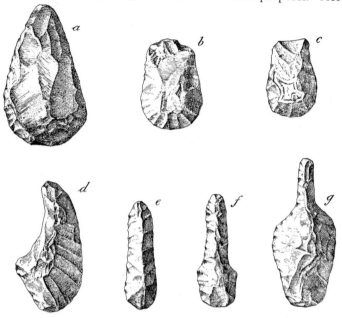

Fig. 352.   Chipped Stone Implements.   Nat. size.
a (₂⁷⁶₀₃), *b* (₂⁰⁴₆₀*a*), *c* (₂⁰⁵₆₀*a*) Scrapers. Kamloops; *d* (₂⁸⁷₄₁), Knife. Kamloops; *e* (₂¹⁸₈₄), *f* (₂¹⁶₈₈), Drills.
Kamloops; *g* (₂⁸⁷₇₂), Drill. Spences Bridge.

Baptiste, implements of this kind were used to rub or scrape small pieces of skin.[1] Some pieces of the metapodial bone of the deer, split or cut lengthwise, were rubbed on all edges, and sharpened to a spatulate shape; others were rubbed on the broken edges of the middle part of the bone, as would have been the case had they been used for skin-scrapers.[2]

For scraping and cutting, the chipped objects shown in Fig. 352, *a–c*, would have been useful.   These are rather flat on one side, showing, besides the bulb of percussion, few if any places where chips have been detached.   The other side is of the shape of a turtle-back, and shows much secondary chipping.   The first of these is made of glassy basalt, the second of chert, the third of opal.   Fig. 352 *d* shows an object similar in shape to the carving-knives used until recently.[3]   It is made of chert.   Fig. 352, *e–g*, illustrates the typical chipped specimens suitable

[1] See Part III, Fig. 52.   [2] Ibid., Fig. 65.   [3] See Part IV, Figs. 125, 126.

for drills or perforators found in this region.   The first of these is made of chert, the second of andesitic lava, the third of glassy basalt.

Pairs of coarse siliceous sandstone arrowshaft-smoothers, like those found at Lytton,[1] were frequently found in the graves.   They vary in length from about two to seven inches.

The object shown in Fig. 353 is part of a larger object made of bone of the whale, but no other fragments of it were found.   It shows at the lower end a rectangular cut, as if a hole had been made through it from edge to edge ; and a groove extends along its edges.   Possibly it was the end of the handle of a war-club, with the hole for a suspending-string and the grooves for receiving a thong for the same purpose, or a string of beads, or similar ornamental objects.

The charred bone object shown in Fig. 354 a is shaped like a staple, and was whittled into shape.   The upper end is blunt, and apparently not worn by use.   The prongs are square on the inside, and rounded on the outer edges.   They are rather sharp.   A similar bone object, much bleached (Fig. 354, b) was found on the surface of the

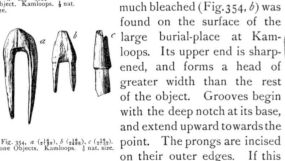

Fig. 353 (₂¹⁸₈₂). Bone Object. Kamloops. ½ nat. size.

Fig. 354, a (₇¹⁸₈ₐ), b (₂¹⁸₈₂), c (₂¹⁸₃₂). Bone Objects. Kamloops. ½ nat. size.

large burial-place at Kamloops.   Its upper end is sharpened, and forms a head of greater width than the rest of the object.   Grooves begin with the deep notch at its base, and extend upward towards the point.   The prongs are incised on their outer edges.   If this

Fig. 355 (₂¹⁸₂ₐ). Skin-scraper. Spences Bridge. ¼ nat. size.

object had originally been slipped over the end of a stick, and bound on, these incisions would have held the winding-strings in place.   These objects may have been points for some implement, parts of dog-harnesses, or attachments of nets. The charred bone object shown in Fig. 354 c was found with the specimen illustrated in Fig. 355, and it shows that it was whittled into shape.   Both ends are broken off, but some of the Indians believe it to be part of a beaver-spear point.

Many implements were found which served for the preparation of skins and for sewing vegetable materials.   Skin-scrapers made of pebbles of quartz,

---

[1] See Part III, p. 146.

argillite, granite, and other materials, were in general like those found at Lytton. The specimen shown in Fig. 355 is unusually large, being over seven inches and a half long. It is made by chipping the edge of a large flake on both sides. A few are dovetail shape. Some large chipped points made of glassy basalt, and similar in shape to the specimens shown in Fig. 331, would have served well for the same purpose.[1]

The scrapers made of bone were practically of the same kind as those from Lytton. Scrapers made of shoulder-blades of large mammals were secured, but none made from a full-length metapodial bone. The specimen shown in Fig. 356, made of the scapula of a deer, was found in the grave at Spences Bridge. The ends still show traces of windings of vegetable fibre; and the whole specimen resembles the scrapers made of horses' ribs, wound at the ends with sagebrush and skin, such as the present Indians use to beam skins.[1] According to Baptiste, the natural grooves in the skin-scrapers and chisels made of the metapodial bones of the deer and elk[2] were used as receptacles for awls, and needles for making mats. When not in use, the whole scraper was wrapped in skin or textile, and the delicate implements were safely carried in its groove.

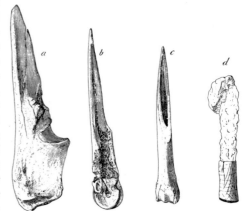

Fig. 356 ($\frac{16}{245}$).
Scraper made of a Scapula. Spences Bridge. ¼ nat. size

Fig. 357. Awls. Kamloops. ½ nat. size.
a ($\frac{16}{400}$), b ($\frac{16}{248}$), c ($\frac{16}{289}$), Bone Awls; d ($\frac{16}{218}$), Iron Awl.

Besides the stone drills or perforators previously mentioned (Fig. 352, e–g), there were found several awls made of bone and one of iron. The specimen shown in Fig. 357 a is made of the proximal part of an ulna of a deer. Another one (Fig. 357, b) is made of one-half of the distal end of the metapodial of a deer. Each of these specimens represents a type of awl, made of a special bone, which is widely distributed in America. The awl shown in Fig. 357 c is made of the distal end of the humerus of a bird, probably a goose or duck, and is cut diagonally across. Fig. 357 d represents an iron awl, with handle made of bone, found in the pouch at the back of the skeleton in the first grave on the Government Hill at Kamloops. The iron shaft is so much oxidized that no trace of metallic iron remains. It is (setting aside the copper, which may be of native origin) the only object suggesting contact with the whites, found at any of the old sites herein

---

[1] See Part IV, p. 185.   [2] See Part III, Figs. 54, 65.

described, except the one west of the mouth of the North Thompson, which was inhabited after the Hudson Bay Company settled there. The bone handle of this specimen is covered with incised lines, probably intended for ornamental purposes, and it is stained by copper salts.

Fine and coarse flat needles made of bone were used throughout the entire region for sewing together cat-tail stalks to form mats, and for other purposes. The specimen shown in Fig. 358 *a* is least flat of all, being nearly half round in cross-section ; and the eye, which in most cases is about a third of the way from the end, is in this case at the tip. It is also connected with the end by what is apparently an accidental crack, but which makes the object resemble a self-threading needle. Another specimen (Fig. 358,*b*) has the eye in the usual place, but it departs from the typical form by being made of a thinner piece of bone, so that it was not rubbed down enough to efface the marrow-canal. The eye is of a circular form, gouged from both sides. Fig. 358 *c* shows the type of bone needle of this region. It has the eye, which is lenticular in form and also cut from both sides, removed more than one-third its length from the end. It is slightly curved, and made of part of a bone so thick that the cellular structure of the inner side is nearly rubbed away. Fig. 358 *d* shows a similar specimen, which has two shallow indentions evidently made purposely,— one near its middle, and the other opposite its eye. The specimen illustrated in Fig. 358 *e* differs from the typical form in having two eyes. One is located slightly nearer the centre than usual ; the other is removed about one-fourth the distance from the end. Fig.

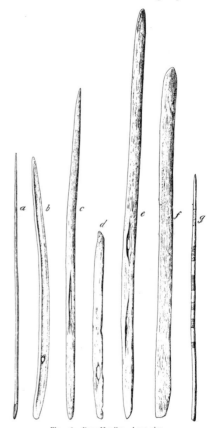

Fig. 358. Bone Needles. ½ nat. size.

a ($\frac{16}{7068}$), *b* ($\frac{16}{7082}$), Nicola Lake ; *c* ($\frac{49}{6373}a$), *d* ($\frac{65}{2683}a$), *e* ($\frac{16}{2081}$), *f* ($\frac{16}{2820}$), *g* ($\frac{16}{2803}$), Kamloops.

358 *f* illustrates a piece of bone evidently intended for a needle, but not yet rubbed down or provided with an eye. The cellular structure of the inner side of the bone is very marked.

The specimen shown in Fig. 358 *g* is of the shape of a knitting-needle. It is made of bone, and shows traces of winding which cover bands separated by five intervals of irregular size. It is slightly colored by red ochre.

A second specimen, bearing four bands, but similar in all other details, was found together with the one described here.

War.—Besides the objects which may have been used in war as well as in hunting (such as chipped points for spears, arrows, and knives), and others that

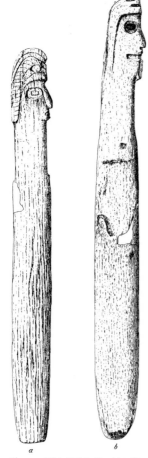

may have been tools as well as weapons (such as club-heads, and the long celts said to have been battle-axes), there are some specimens which were probably useful only in warfare. Prominent among these were three large clubs found at Kamloops. They are made from the rib-bones of the whale. They vary from about nineteen inches to two feet in length. For the greater part of their length they are like the natural bone, lenticular in cross-section. The handle occupies nearly, if not quite, the upper third of the object ; and on two of the specimens (Fig. 359) the knob of the handle is carved to represent a human head, adorned with what is apparently a feather head-dress. The carvings are practically bilaterally symmetrical. The feather head-dress may be clearly recognized in the smaller club (Fig. 359, *a*), the beak forming a crest over the human face. The eye in this crest may belong to the bird from the skin of which the head-dress is made, or the whole may be a head-mask. The lips of the human figure are apart, and the tongue is pushed forward between them. The specimen shown in Fig. 359 *b* is the largest of the three clubs, and retains the lateral curve of the rib. The carving, while less intricate than that on the smaller specimen, is quite as striking. The former specimen shows distinct marks of the handle having been wound with cord. The winding probably served to give a better hold, and ended in a loop by which the club was suspended from the wrist.[1]   A fourth club, not carved, but made of the same material, is in the provincial Museum at Victoria. It was col-

Fig. 359, *a* (₂₁₀₈₅), *b* (₂₁₀₈₄). War-clubs. Kamloops. ¼ nat. size.

lected at Kamloops, in 1893, by Mr. C. G. King. The whole style of carving of these clubs suggests imitation of the art of the Coast tribes, from whose territory the material for the objects came. Bone clubs as narrow as this, or with handles of this type, have not been found on the coast. The general style of the carving of these handles is most closely approached on the southeastern part of Vancouver Island, but there the carving usually represents a bird's head.

[1] See Part IV, p. 263.

A dagger or knife over one foot long, made of antler, was found in excavating at the large burial-place at Kamloops. It does not vary materially from a similar specimen found at Lytton,[1] except in having a hole through the upper end. This hole is about a quarter of an inch long, and of the shape of a rectangle with rounded corners. It seems to be worn, as if a thong had been passed through it.

The specimen shown in Fig. 360 *a* is rudely made of the thin edge of some large bone, such as a scapula. It has a sharp point. The handle is roughly broken, but may have been wound with bark twine. It is notched near its end, and a scratched groove extends across it from the notch. This notch may have served for holding in place skin or fabric wound around it for a handle, or it may have been simply for attaching a string for suspension. Possibly the implement served as a knife, to be used for a variety of purposes. Fig. 360 *b* shows a beautifully ornamented dagger or spear point made of antler. Its base is much decomposed, but a circular perforation may still be seen. It is lenticular in cross-section. Iron-Head said that formerly such implements, made of antler, frequently served as spear-points.

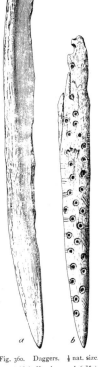

Dress and Ornament.—Skins of the deer, birds, and other animals, have been found in the graves, and were evidently portions of garments and pouches. No spindle whorls have been found above Lytton. No evidence was found that mountain-goat wool and dog-hair were spun and woven.

Fragments of fabrics woven from vegetable fibre were found at all the sites. Such material was probably used in this region for much of the clothing, as well as for pouches, mats, etc.

Mats, which were sometimes found as outer wrappings on the bodies in the graves, were made of cat-tail stalks, either sewed or woven together.[2] The vegetable fibre used in sewing and weaving these stalks, and in weaving in general, was probably similar to that used by the present Indians.[3] Most of the fabrics found in the graves were too fragmentary for determination. Sewed matting was over the burial-tent in the first Nicola Valley grave, while one of the bodies at the Government Hill Site at Kamloops was wrapped in woven matting. Mats were probably used in much the same way as they are by the present Indians. Food is spread on them to dry. They serve many purposes as a piece of household furniture, such as rugs, table-mats, and bedding ; and they are used for covering lodges. The bodies, after being wrapped in mats, were sometimes bound with a three-stranded cord, about one-fourth of an

a   *b*

Fig. 360.   Daggers.   ¼ nat. size.
a (₁₀⁹₃), Kamloops ; *b* (₇₁⁹₀).
Nicola Lake.

---

[1] See Part III, Fig. 80.   [2] See Part IV, Fig. 131, *c, e.*   [3] *Ibid.*, p. 188 *ff.*

inch in diameter, made of fibre resembling cedar-bark. The small strands were made by twisting the fibre to the left, and these were combined by twisting to the right. Pouches such as were found with the skeletons and other portions of fabric were similar in all details to the fabrics illustrated in Fig. 131, *d* and *h*, Part IV. Other pieces were made of the same weave as that shown in Fig. 131, *e* or *b*, but of much finer strands. Some have a finer warp but a coarse woof. The coarser strands of the warp are probably very small rushes. Fibres resembling straw, grass, or in some cases the rough outer bark of the elm, were found in these fabrics, the weight of the soil apparently having pressed two distinct layers together. These fibres seem not to have been woven. It is possible that these were mattings made of cat-tails, and that only pieces between the stitches happen to be preserved. Flat pieces of fibrous matter were found which resemble sheets of pounded bark, and which in structure are somewhat like bark-cloth. There were also black fibres of bark found in rolls, and many shreds of cedar-bark. Such may have served as slow-matches for carrying fire. Shredded cedar-bark was found near the heads of some of the bodies, and may have served as pillows or bedding for the bodies. Fragments of such bark are still attached to the arrow-shaft shown in Fig. 338 *b*.

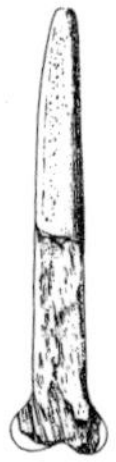

Personal ornaments in great variety were found. Red, yellowish-red, and yellow ochre, copper clay, and charcoal were frequently met with, and, mixed with grease, probably served for painting the body. The pieces of copper clay show rubbed surfaces. They were probably ground on stone in preparing paint. Body and clothing were further decorated with ornaments of the same materials as were employed at Lytton. No combs were found. Objects made of stone and bone were secured, that the Indians believed to have been head-scratchers. The specimen shown in Fig. 361 is one of these, and is made of beautiful white aragonite. It seems that it had two lobes, which, however, are broken away. The specimen was formed by rubbing, and may have been a head-scratcher or a hair or nose ornament.[1] The specimen shown in Fig. 362, however, is more likely to have served as a head-scratcher.[2] It is made of bone, and bears an incised design.

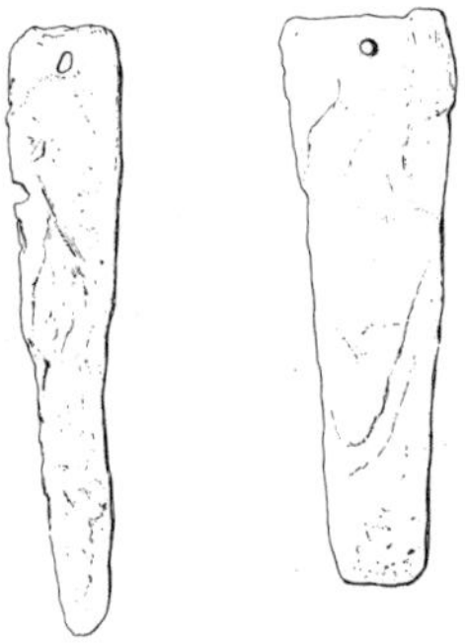

Fig. 361.

Fig. 364. Fig. 362. Fig. 363.

Fig. 361 (₂₁₄₀). Stone Object. Kamloops. ½ nat. size.
Fig. 362 (₂₁₈₈). Head-scratcher. Kamloops. ½ nat. size.
Fig 363 (₇₆₈₂), (₇₆₈₃). Copper Pendants. Nicola Lake. ½ nat. size.
Fig. 364 (₂₆₀₈). Copper Pendant. Kamloops. ½ nat. size.

---

[1] See Part IV, p. 223.

[2] Ibid., p. 312.

The pendants shown in Fig. 363 are made of thin copper, each with a small irregular hole punched in the wide end. They were found near the neck of a skeleton. The copper disk shown in Fig. 364 has a small perforation, and was probably a pendant for the ear.

With the copper objects shown in Fig. 363, others (Figs. 365, 366) were found in a mass near the neck of a skeleton. The last-named figure shows what is unmistakably a neck-lace of four strands of shell beads of cylin-drical form, about an eighth of an inch in diameter, and about a thirty-second of an inch in thickness, with a bore of about a thirty-second of an inch. These are strung on a cord made of vegetable fibre twisted to the left. The loops meet, and are held at the back by a cord, which is also twisted to the left. Suspended from the middle of the front was a perforated copper pendant, a fragment of which remains. Its shape resembled that of the pendants shown in Fig. 365, and Figs. 87-89, Part III. The testimony of Charlie Tcilaxitca in regard to these specimens agrees with the finds. He said that they were probably worn on the chest by the daughters of chiefs.

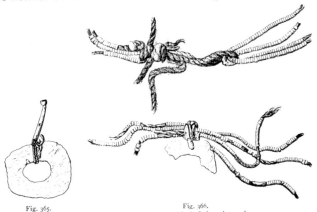

Fig. 365.

Fig. 366.

Fig. 365 (₇⁷₂²₁). Copper Pendant. Nicola Lake. ½ nat. size.
Fig. 366 (₇⁷₀¹₉). Necklace. Nicola Lake. ¼ nat. size.

One of these pendants (Fig. 365) is suspended by a string the strands of which are twisted to the right, but other strands, noticeable in the knot, are twisted to the left. The string is tied twice around the pendant through the large central opening. It then passes up through a whole dentalium shell and through a small cylindrical bead made of vegetable material. As the necklace near which this piece was found had a pendant, it seems probable that this speci-men may have been used for an ear-ornament, especially since another specimen found in the same grave matches it, and dentalium shells and beads found loose near by may have been similarly attached to that specimen.

Some fragments of mica that were found may have been fastened to the garments for ornamental purposes. In Fig. 367 is illustrated a pendant made of bone, found in a pouch at the back of a body. It is colored yellowish red by the ochre in the grave. The two edges are rounded, and the ends are sharp like those of a sap-scraper. The perforation, which is rather large, is gouged from both sides, and the surface of the specimen is scratched with crude lines. Its shape and size are so closely related to the copper pendants that they suggest its use for a similar purpose, although it may have served as a sap-scraper.

The nail or outer covering of a bear-claw, cut across at the upper end, through which an elliptical eye was gouged for receiving a skin thong, was found in a mass of material at the neck of a skeleton. Another pendant (Fig. 368) was made of the core of a bear's claw. It also has been cut across and perforated at the upper end. The hole is crudely drilled from both sides. The palm side of this claw is scraped or cut. All of the pendants made of cores of bears' claws had been burned. Some cores of puma claws were found in the graves at the large burial-place at Kamloops. One of them shows incised lines across it, but others remain in their natural form.

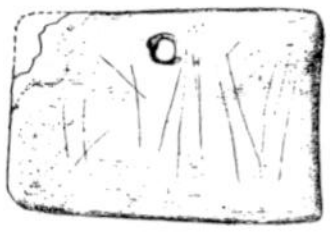

Fig. 367. 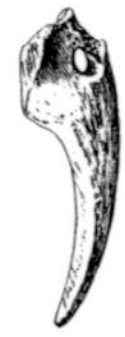   Fig. 368.    Fig. 369.    Fig. 370.

Fig. 367 (₂¹⁰₈ₙ). Bone Pendant. Kamloops. ½ nat. size.
Fig. 368 (₂⁴⁶₆₈₅). Pendant made of Bear's Claw. Kamloops. ½ nat. size.
Fig. 369 (₂¹⁰₈ₙ). Pendant made of Incisor of Deer. Kamloops. ½ nat. size.
Fig. 370 (₂¹¹₁₀ᵈ). Bone Bead. Kamloops. ⅛ nat. size.

In Fig. 369 is illustrated one of the many pendants made of the incisor of a deer, and found at the neck of a skeleton. A perforation is drilled from both sides through the root of the tooth. This specimen, like many of those found, is stained by copper salts. Along with these pendants made of incisor teeth, and also throughout the region, were found pendants made of the canine teeth of the elk, that are exactly like those found at Lytton.[1] According to Charlie Tcilaxitca, pendants made of teeth, like those referred to here,[2] were used one for each ear, as well as in larger numbers on a string for necklaces.

A small piece of abelone shell with smooth edges was found in the grave at Spences Bridge. It shows part of a perforation, and may have been a portion of a pendant. No specimens made of abelone shell have been found by us farther to the east than Spences Bridge.

Beads for necklaces, ear-ornaments, fringes, and the like, were made of copper, shell, bone, and vegetable material. Many flat bone beads (Fig. 370) of irregular shape, but somewhat rectangular with rounded corners, were found with cremated bones at the Government Site and on the surface at the large burial-place at Kamloops. Many of these beads were charred. They were generally perforated near the centre, the hole tapering from each side in the usual way. Strips of flat copper were rolled into tubes from seven-eighths of an inch to an inch and a half in length. Many of these were used as beads, as is proved by finding them strung with other beads. Some of the longer specimens, however,

---

[1] See Part III, Fig. 96.   [2] See also *ibid.*, Figs. 96–98.

may have served as nose-ornaments, to be inserted horizontally through a hole in the nasal septum.

Fig. 371 shows the use of the rolls of copper in combination with dentalium shells for necklaces. These beads are strung on strings made of fibre, some of which are twisted to the right. A small fragment of this ornament shows dentalium shells arranged on small cords twisted to the left. There is a cord at right angles to the shells which serves to keep the strings apart. This specimen is probably a portion of a large breast-shield, the rest of which had fallen to pieces. Numerous dentalium shells found in the same grave were prob-

Fig. 371 ($\frac{16}{279}$). String of Copper and Dentalium Beads. Kamloops. ½ nat. size.

ably parts of this ornament. Such breast-shields are frequently seen among the present Indians of the North Pacific coast. In the graves at the large burial-place at Kamloops some dentalium shells were found which bear incised designs. These designs are shown in Fig. 379. The objects were probably nose-ornaments, ear-pendants, or parts of ornaments similar to that last mentioned.

Besides simple shell beads made from sections of dentalium shells cut from about a thirty-second of an inch to an eighth of an inch in length, there were also found on the surface of the large burial-place at Kamloops perforated disks or short cylinders of shell described as approximately an eighth of an inch in diameter, a thirty-second of an inch thick or long, with a bore a thirty-second of an inch in diameter. These are drilled from each side in the usual manner, tapering towards the centre. There are also beads similar to these, but of about twice the diameter, and with a much less tapering perforation. From the surface of the Government Hill a number of beads were secured, each made of a basal ring of a barnacle. The ends and edges had been rubbed to give the beads a somewhat symmetrical form. No beads made of olivella shells were found.

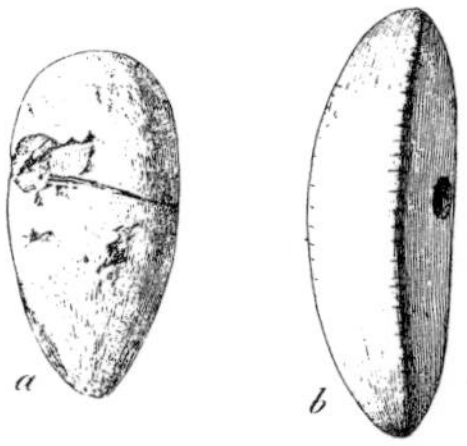

The object shown in Fig. 372 a is made of fluorite, has an almond shape with one side flat, while over the curved upper side a groove is cut not far above the middle of the object. Fig. 372 b shows another stone object. It is well worked on all surfaces, and apparently polished by use. A perforation, as usual tapering from each end towards the middle, extends through it from side to side. The base is flat, and the ends rather sharp. The entire object is square in cross-section, except that the upper corners are rounded and their edges notched. It suggests at once the bird-shaped stones of the Mississippi Valley, which Cushing believed were used in the head-dress. According to information obtained by Mr. Teit from Indians at Spences Bridge,

Fig. 372, a ($\frac{16}{2002}$), b ($\frac{16}{2690}$). Stone Objects. Kamloops. ½ nat. size.

this object (and probably the former one also) may have been an attachment to a dog-halter, or, which they thought far more likely, a sinker for a fish-line.

Games, Amusements, Narcotics. — Sets of dice made of beaver-teeth, similar to those found at Lytton,[1] but varying in the details of the number of incised marks and circular pits on them, were frequently found in the graves. The game played with these has continued in use among many tribes of this territory until the present day, and is consequently well known.[2]

The astragalus bone of the deer[3] is often found in the sites of the Thompson River region, and may have been used, as it is farther east, as a dice.

Tubes made of bird-bone, varying in length from an inch and a half to two inches and a half, and of proportionate diameters, were found in the pouches in graves. Five were found in one bag, and one in another, so that their number does not seem significant. They were all colored by red ochre. Some of them bear a few notches or are slightly scratched; but no design is noticed except on one, which has upon one side a row of diagonal scratches, and on the other a double row of zigzag lines with five angles. Some of the specimens show that the end of the bone was partly cut through and then broken off; others are cut smoothly. The ends of all the tubes are fairly square. These may have been used as gambling-bones.[4]

There were found in the pouches in the grave at Spences Bridge, and in Nicola Valley, cylinders or oval bars of bone and wood about an inch and a half long. Four of these, made of bone, were found together in the grave at Spences Bridge. All are marked with incised lines. Three of them are shown in Fig. 373. The reverse sides of *a* and *b* bear only transverse incisions. One made of wood, found in the second grave at the eastern end of Nicola Lake, is hollow. The bark is still on, and it has several notches on each side.

Some whole shells of *Pecten caurinus* were found at the large burial-place at Kamloops. Each is perforated by an oval hole about half an inch long, cut through the flat valve about half an inch from the central apex of the shell, below the ligamental pit. These are evidently parts of rattles similar to those used in the dances of the present Coast Indians.

Fig. 373 (₂₈₄₄₀).
Gambling-bones.
Spences Bridge. ½ nat. size.

The stone pipes (Fig. 374) found in graves at the large burial-place at Kamloops resemble in general those of Lytton. They are made from steatite, are of tubular form, with a bowl the shape of a wine-glass. In the first specimen (Fig. 374, *a*) the tube for half an inch from the mouth is larger than the shaft, and forms a mouthpiece which shows traces of windings. The present Indians sometimes wind the mouthpieces of their pipes with string, that they may the easier hold them with their teeth. The shaft has been broken near its junction with the bowl, and here also are stains

<hr>

[1] See Part III, Fig. 100.
[2] See *ibid.*, p. 153; Part IV, p. 272.
[3] See Part III, Fig. 101.
[4] See Part IV, p. 275.

as of windings.   Possibly it had been repaired in this way.   The stem is marked off from the bowl by three carved rings.   The bowl is small in proportion to the stem, and is cut squarely across at the edge.   It is broken.   It contains a mass of carbonaceous matter which yields ammonia on distillation.   The large ash residue is alumina and silica.   Another pipe made of mottled green steatite (Fig. 374, b) is highly polished, and the bowl is ornamented with incised lines. The edge of the bowl is sharp, and the whole receptacle is large in proportion to the stem, which is separated from it by two carved rings.   The stem was hollowed by drilling from both ends.   These drillings did not meet squarely, and the side of the stem was broken in consequence.   From the mouth to the middle of the stem the hole is slightly funnel-shaped.   No pipes were found by us at Spences Bridge or in Nicola Valley.   The modern pipes of the whole region are not tubular.[1]   Chief Salicte at Nicola Lake said that the narrow-leaved tobacco (*Nicotiana attenuata* Torr.) of the region was used pure until the manufactured tobacco was introduced.   Not until then were the leaves of bearberry (*Arctostaphylos uva-ursi* Spreng.) mixed with tobacco.

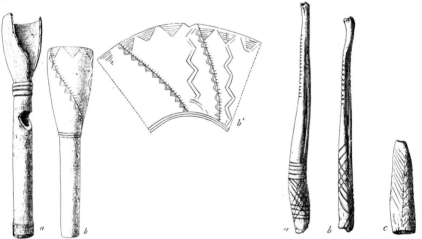

Fig. 374, *a* (₂¹⁴₁₀), *b* (₂¹⁴₁₂).   Stone Pipes.   Kamloops.   ½ nat. size.
b' Developed design on bowl of *b*.

Fig. 375, *a* (₂¹⁴₂), *b* (₂¹⁴₇), *c* (₂¹⁴₁).   Bone
Carvings.   Kamloops.   ½ nat. size.

These tubular pipes penetrated to the coast.   A fragment of one was found in a shell-heap at Port Hammond.   A piece of a very large one was found in a shell-heap at North Saanich, and a perfect short-stemmed specimen was seen at the shell-heap near Sidney.

A chalcedony concretion of conoid shape was found in a grave at the eastern end of Nicola Lake.   It may have been a charm, or valued on account of its attractive form.

---

[1] See Part IV, Fig. 271.

Art.—The graphic and plastic arts of the early people of this region are illustrated by engravings and carvings in bone and stone, antler, and on dentalium shells. Many of the objects found in the graves are colored by red ochre.

The engravings closely resemble the painted designs of the present Indians, who are able to interpret them by analogy with their own designs.[1] The digging-stick handles made of antler are ornamented by incised lines.[2] Long lines with short marks at right angles to them are often found. Sometimes the short marks are wide and deep at the base, and taper to a point, forming minute triangular pyramids resting on the long line. These markings probably represent the manitous of the owners of the objects. There are numerous pieces of bone and antler with incised cross-lines and notches or the sides. Awls are frequently marked with notches along the sides. The engravings on the pipe mentioned above (Fig. 374, *b'*) also consist of lines.

In two specimens of the penis-bone of the bear, which had been decorated by incised lines and notches, there is an eye, similar to the eyes in the bone needles, cut longitudinally from both sides through the lower portion of the bone (Fig. 375, *a*, *b*).

Fig. 375 *c* shows a piece of antler of conoid shape, with the tip cut squarely across. It is colored by red ochre found with it, and is slightly worn. From base to tip extend three rows of incised lines, each like an inverted letter V, placed one over the other at a distance of about one-eighth of an inch. According to information secured from the Indians by Mr. Teit, these may represent wood-worm borings.

The bone object shown in Fig. 376 has the form of an ellipse with broken ends, and bent to a crescent shape. The edges are rounded and smooth. In the middle of its outer surface, extending lengthwise of the specimen, is an incised design similar to a ladder. Seven cross-lines show, some having been broken away with the ends of the specimen, which are lacking. A specimen similar in shape has been found in a shell-heap at North Saanich.

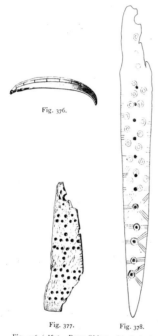

Fig. 376.

Fig. 377.   Fig. 378.

Fig. 376 (₂₅₆₆°). Bone Object with Incised Design. Kamloops. ½ nat. size.

Fig. 377 (₂₄₆₀°). Sap-scraper. Spences Bridge. ½ nat. size.

Fig. 378 (₇₆₃₀). Dagger with Incised Design. Kamloops. ½ nat. size.

Fig. 377 represents a delicate bone sap-scraper with a perforation at the top for suspension. It is decorated by drilled pits artistically arranged. There are also a few notches along one edge.

The dagger described on p. 423 is ornamented with circles, circular pits, and incised lines. Most of the lines extend over the edge of the dagger to the other

---

[1] See Part III, p. 156; Part IV, p. 378.   [2] See Part III, Fig. 21.

side, connecting some of the circles and pits. This is shown in Fig. 378, in which the ornamentation on the reverse of the dagger is drawn in broken lines.

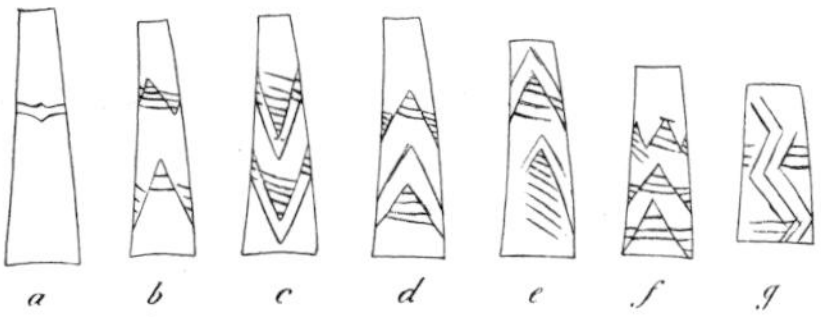

Some of the dentalium shells found in a grave at the large burial-place at Kamloops bear incised designs, which are shown in Fig. 379.

Fig. 379 ($\frac{18}{2885}$). Incised Designs from Dentalium Shells. Kamloops. ½ nat. size.

Fig. 380 ($\frac{16}{1663}$). Stone Image. Kamloops. ½ nat. size. (Drawn from a cast, original in the Provincial Museum, Victoria, B. C., formerly owned by Mr. C. Hill-Tout.)

The most artistic carvings found in this region are the specimens shown in Figs. 359, *a*, *b*, and 380.[1] The last-named specimen represents a human head surmounted by a human figure. There is a conoid-shaped hole resembling a pipe-bowl in the forehead of the lower figure. On the back of the upper figure is a sculpture in relief, suggesting a lizard without legs. Between the throat of this figure and the back of the human figure there is a perforation made by two cone-shaped holes meeting from each side. This specimen resembles in a general way certain stone carvings found on southeastern Vancouver Island, in the Lillooet Valley north of Harrison Lake, and in the vicinity of Yale, B. C. All these specimens bear a certain resemblance to sculptures of the region of Columbia River, the Gulf of Georgia, and Puget Sound, and may have originated under the influence of the culture of these districts.

Fig. 381 (²⁶⁷⁵). Carved Tip of Antler. Kamloops. ½ nat. size.

Fig. 381 shows the tip of an antler which is carved to represent the head and neck of a bird. The mouth is indicated by a long furrow on each side, while each eye is represented by a drilled cone-shaped hole. The specimen is charred.

Method of Burial.—The dead were evidently buried at a short distance from the villages. No burials were found in any of the pits marking the sites of underground houses. In most cases the bodies were buried in the ground, apparently at a depth of about three feet. The knees were drawn up to the chin, and in some cases evidence was found that the body was wrapped in fabrics or mats, and then tied up with cords. Traces of red ochre and other paints on the bones and in the earth surrounding the skeleton give evidence either that the body was painted before burial, or that paints were buried with it. The body was also decorated with the ornaments of the deceased, such as ear-pendants, nose-ornament, necklaces, etc. His tools were buried with him. Some were often put in a pouch, which seems to have been placed near the middle of the

[1] See the B. C. Mining Record, Christmas number, 1899, where the same specimen is described by Mr. C. Hill-Tout.

body.   In these pouches were found arrow-makers' tools, such as pieces of glassy basalt, finished arrow-points and shaft-smoothers ; and also gambling-implements, such as dice made of beaver-teeth.   Graves of women contained their tools, such as needles for mat-making and awls.

In a few cases the grave was surrounded by a number of poles or by slabs of wood.   It would seem that small tents were erected over the body, which gradually decayed, leaving only the butt-ends of the poles, which were buried in the sand.   One of the graves at Kamloops was found surrounded by pieces of a broken canoe arranged in the form of a conical tent over it (see Plate XXVI). Only the lower parts of the pieces of wood were preserved.   It would seem that after the tent had been erected, the sand was blown into it, and the lower part of the wood was covered, and thus protected from the weather.   Three graves near the mouth of Nicola Lake were covered with a few bowlders.   There is evidence that these three graves are of recent origin.   One of them is known to have been made between 1840 and 1850.   The evidence afforded by the finds as described here, agrees closely with the description of modern burial-customs of the Thompson Indians given by Mr. Teit.[1]

In Nicola Valley a number of graves were found in rock-slides.   In these the skeletons, with few exceptions, were placed on the back, with knees doubled up, the head towards the east.   A remarkable number of large celts of nephrite, a number of well-preserved copper pendants, and a necklace were found here. The bodies were covered by disturbing the rock-slides and allowing some of the material to fall down over them.   It would seem that a few rocks were placed on the tops of the graves in order to mark the sites.   Besides this, poles or branches were put up over the graves.   One of these graves was also covered by a small tent made of poles that had been covered with mats.   Near some of these bodies were found skeletons of dogs.   Their bones were colored here and there with red ochre, and the rocks close by were also colored from contact with lumps of paint.

At the Government Site near Kamloops a number of small masses of children's bones were found.   The bones in all of these were partly burned, and with them were many bone beads, chipped cache forms of glassy basalt, etc. They were found less than six inches deep, while some of the bones were on the surface.   It is possible that these were uncovered by the wind.

Near Kamloops a considerable number of caches were found which contained pieces of glassy basalt and hammer-stones, while in others were bone awls, needles, sap-scrapers, etc.   These caches were not associated with any graves.[2]

Conclusion.—The finds made at Kamloops, Spences Bridge, and in Nicola Valley, corroborate the conclusions drawn from archæological investigation of the burial-ground at Lytton.   The ancient culture of the whole of the southern interior of British Columbia was quite uniform, and resembled in all essential

---

[1] Part IV, pp. 328, 329.

[2] A detailed account of the material found in the graves and caches will be found in the Appendix, pp. 434 *ff.*

points the culture of the present inhabitants of this area, as described by James Teit in his monograph on the Thompson Indians.   It has been pointed out that this culture shows close affinities to that of the interior of Oregon and of California, and that on the whole its affiliations are rather with the tribes of the Plains than with those of the North Pacific coast.   Nevertheless there is evidence that the Coast people have influenced the culture of the interior of British Columbia.   Material such as shells and bone of the whale, from which utensils and implements were made, was imported from the coast, and some of the carvings of this region may perhaps be considered as made by artists familiar with the art of the Coast Indians.

The physical type of the people of the interior is quite uniform, and a preliminary examination of the skeletons of the prehistoric people does not suggest that any change of type has taken place.   Measurements of the living show a certain amount of mixture with the Coast type to have extended some distance up Fraser River, but beyond this point there is a fundamental difference between the types of the coast and those of the interior, the former being characterized by broad faces and large heads, while the latter have narrow faces and small heads.   Therefore it may be said that both culture and physical type suggest that the peoples of the coast and those of the interior developed on distinct lines, and that points of resemblance are due to later contact.

APPENDIX I.

LIST AND CATALOGUE NUMBERS OF SURFACE FINDS, AND CONTENTS OF GRAVES AND CACHES, UPON WHICH THE PRECEDING DESCRIPTION IS BASED.

SPENCES BRIDGE.

$\frac{16}{1286}$, $\frac{16}{2870}-\frac{16}{2882}$, $\frac{16}{4557}$, $\frac{16}{5650}-\frac{16}{5661}$, $\frac{16}{6981}-\frac{16}{6983}$. Surface finds. (See Figs. 332 *e*, *h*, 334 *a*, 335 *b*, 341 *c*, 352 *g*, 355.)

$\frac{16}{2832}-\frac{16}{2869}$. Grave 22 inches below the surface. In the soil above it were a number of bowlders, such as are common along the river. Below these, at a depth of 6 inches, were rolls of birch-bark about half an inch in diameter,[1] and some fragments of charcoal. Several of the bowlders showed signs of having been in contact with fire. Extending around the grave at intervals of about a foot were charred remains of posts, approximately an inch and a half in diameter. They were still standing upon end, but did not extend above the surface, the projecting portions, if there had been any, having been destroyed.

The body was that of a man about forty-five years of age. It was buried face downward, with head towards the south. The knees were slightly flexed, so that the feet, knees, and pelvis formed the corners of an equilateral triangle, the feet lying in line with the vertebral column. The right arm extended under the chest to the left elbow, and the left hand reached across below the pelvis. The body was entirely wrapped in a fabric woven of the inner bark of the sagebrush, outside of which was a mat or blanket of cat-tail stalks made by weaving rather than stitching. The entire bundle was bound with a cord about a fourth of an inch in diameter. With the body were the following objects :—

A pair of grooved arrowshaft-smoothers at the left elbow, near a pouch made of woven vegetable fibre, which extended from the left elbow to the left knee, was daubed with red ochre, and contained a bone scraper wound at the ends with vegetable fibre ; red ochre ; jaw of a rodent ; a bundle of bone implements, one of which was rubbed at the end ; five bone cylinders ; two teeth ; chipped points and pieces of glassy basalt ; a bone pendant ; two fish vertebræ ; part of a beaver's lower jaw ; three pieces of beaver-teeth ; the beak of a great blue heron ; a beak of another bird ; caudal vertebræ of a small mammal ; pieces of wood, one probably being an arrow-shaft ; an arrowshaft-smoother ; seven bone objects, some of them showing traces of winding, and all evidently parts of harpoon-points ; pieces of antler and bone, some of the latter being sharpened ; a skin-scraper made of bone. Six chips of glassy basalt, a piece of perforated abelone shell with smoothed edges, pieces of beaver-teeth, and a long copper bead or tube, were found by Mr. Teit when he discovered this grave by digging into it. (See Figs. 336 *c*, *e*, 338 *b*, 356, 373, 377.)

LARGE BURIAL-PLACE AT KAMLOOPS.

$\frac{16}{2414}-\frac{16}{2442}$, $\frac{16}{2783}$, $\frac{16}{2830}$, $\frac{16}{4982}-\frac{16}{4992}$, $\frac{16}{5015}$, $\frac{16}{6950}-\frac{16}{6956}$. Surface finds. (See Figs. 333 *c*, 341 *a*, 350 *a*, 361, 380.)

$\frac{16}{2443}-\frac{16}{2869}$. Objects which, although distinctly found in graves, were not identified with particular skeletons. (See Figs. 331 *a*, 332 *d*, 337 *c*, 351 *b*, 352 *f*, 354 *b*, 359 *a*, *b*.)

The remains of skeletons obtained from the following graves were usually found at a depth of about 3 feet. So far as could be distinguished, the bodies had been buried on the side, with

---

[1] See Part III, Fig. 117.

knees drawn up to the chest. The bones were much decayed. In some cases it was even impossible to distinguish a single bone, as the whole skeleton was decomposed to a mass resembling sawdust. This may be due to the fact that the land bordering the river is low, so that the lower layers of sand are always wet.

$\frac{16}{2601}-\frac{16}{2611}$. Grave 1 (objects found as if they had been buried in a pouch). — 2 pairs arrowshaft-smoothers made of sandstone ; 1 rubbed stone ; 4 whetstones ; 2 broken skin-scrapers made of deer-bone ; 1 fragment of bone showing artificial shaping ; 1 notched bone ; 8 sharp bone implements ; 3 pieces of pecten shell ; 25 pieces of chipped glassy basalt, including arrow-points, etc. ; and fragments of bark. (See Figs. 336 d, f–h, 376.)

$\frac{16}{2612}-\frac{16}{2618}$. Grave 2. — Stone pipe ornamented with incised lines ; 2 large whetstones ; 3 small whetstones ; 1 rubbed slate point ; a piece of mica ; a piece of red ochre ; 9 chipped pieces of glassy basalt, some of them forming rude arrow-points. (See Figs. 335 a, 351 a, 374 b.)

$\frac{16}{2619}-\frac{16}{2626}$. Grave 3. — A broken stone pipe ; a large white chalcedony chipped point ; 1 chipped point ; 9 chips of glassy basalt ; dentalium shells ; 1 piece of copper clay ; charcoal. (See Figs. 333 a, 374 a.)

$\frac{16}{2627}-\frac{16}{2636}$. Grave 4. — 2 carved penis-bones of the bear ; 1 bone awl ; 4 bone needles ; birch-bark ; bark ; charcoal ; 31 chips of glassy basalt ; dentalium shells ; fragments of bone. (See Figs. 358 d, 375 a, b.)

$\frac{16}{2637}-\frac{16}{2643}$. Grave 5. — 1 stone hammer ; 1 pair arrowshaft-smoothers ; 3 pieces chipped glassy basalt ; 1 whetstone ; copper clay ; a piece of carved antler bearing copper stains ; 1 bone implement. (See Fig. 341 b.)

$\frac{16}{2644}-\frac{16}{2653}$. Grave 6 (close to Grave 5). — 2 pieces of copper ; 1 bone awl ; 2 bone implements ; dentalia beads ; fragments of antler and human bones ; 1 arrowshaft-smoother ; 1 chipped point ; a stone knife ; 6 pieces of chipped glassy basalt.

$\frac{16}{2654}-\frac{16}{2656}$. Grave 7 (near Grave 5). — 3 chipped points ; 1 chipped piece of chert ; dentalia beaus.

$\frac{16}{2657}-\frac{16}{2665}$. Grave 8. — Dentalia beads ; a carved bone awl ; fragments of bone ; a bone imple-ment ; a roll of birch-bark ; 2 nephrite celts ; a large whetstone ; a stone implement. (See Fig. 362.)

$\frac{16}{2666}-\frac{16}{2684}$. Grave 9. — Cylindrical shell beads ; a burned bone awl ; a piece of galena ; 5 pieces of copper clay ; a slate fish-knife ; chips of chalcedony ; a fragment of a stone pipe ; a small celt of green stone ; 5 chipped scrapers of glassy basalt ; 7 chipped points of glassy basalt, six of them being leaf-shaped ; 1 chipped point of chalcedony ; 1 stone ; 2 chips of glassy basalt ; 1 chip of stone ; 1 little arrow-point ; piece of object made of bone of whale ; a bone tube ; burned bones, some of which were human. (See Figs. 332 a, 333 b, 344, 350 b, 353.)

$\frac{16}{2685}-\frac{16}{2691}$. Grave 10. — Dentalium shells, some bearing incised designs ; a large chipped point ; burned bone ; 7 chipped points ; 4 chips of glassy basalt ; red ochre. (See Figs. 332 g, i, j, 379.)

$\frac{16}{2692}-\frac{16}{2705}$. Grave 11. — 2 pieces of sandstone ; copper clay ; 2 whetstones ; 2 claws ; a beaver-tooth ; a bear's canine tooth ; fragments of pecten shells ; dentalium shells ; a celt made of nephrite ; 16 chips and chipped points of glassy basalt ; bone implements ; copper disk. (See Figs. 340 a, 364.)

$\frac{99}{2602}, \frac{16}{6957}-\frac{16}{6979}$. Grave 12 (partly uncovered by the wind ; the skeleton, that of a man about fifty years of age, lay flexed, on the left side). — 2 pairs of arrowshaft-smoothers ; 2 rubbed stones ; 2 pieces of galena ; 2 pieces of yellow paint ; 1 piece of copper clay ; 4 cache forms ; 32 chips, 2 pieces, and 4 points of glassy basalt ; 2 chipped chert scrapers ; a wedge of antler ; a bone needle ; pieces of bone, some of which are cut ; a broken harpoon-point of antler ;

a rubbed bone point ; 4 pieces of beaver-teeth ; a fresh-water unio shell ; various objects of bone and antler. (See Figs. 333 *d*, 337 *a*, 358 *c*.)

$\frac{16}{2606}-\frac{16}{2609}$. Grave 13 (a child).—Dentalium shells, pieces of shell, refuse.

$\frac{16}{4993}-\frac{16}{4999}$. Cache about 6 inches deep and 200 feet from the river.—Bone implements, a bone awl, and 3 sap-scrapers made of bone. (See Figs. 339 *a*, *b*, 357 *a*, 360 *a*.)

GOVERNMENT SITE, NEAR KAMLOOPS.

All of the human bones found here were partly burned, and some were stained by copper salts. The surface of this site resembled that of the large burial-ground. Flat bone beads were numerous with some of the masses of burned bones.

$\frac{16}{2625}-\frac{16}{2643}, \frac{16}{2689}, \frac{16}{5000}-\frac{16}{5011}, \frac{16}{6949}$. Surface finds. (See Figs. 346, 352 *b–d*.)

$\frac{16}{2644}-\frac{16}{2658}$. Cache near following cremated remains, but not distinctly associated with them (depth, 6 inches).—A stone mortar inverted over a chip and three chipped points of glassy basalt, a bone drinking-tube, a bone needle with two eyes, three bone awls, a beaver-tooth dice, a beaver-tooth and other bone implements. (See Figs. 342, 357 *b*, 358 *e*, *f*.)

$\frac{16}{2659}-\frac{16}{2666}$. Charred human bones No. 1 (original depth, judging from topography, about 1 ft., partly uncovered by wind), remains of a child ; 51 chipped triangular cache forms of glassy basalt ; a rubbed stone ; fragments of chipped implements ; a fluorite object of almond shape ; an incised antler-tip ; cylindrical beads made of dentalium shells ; burned oblong flat bone beads. (See Figs. 331 *b*, 372 *a*.)

$\frac{16}{2667}-\frac{16}{2688}$. Charred human bones No. 2 (found about 30 ft. south of No. 1, and barely covered with sand) ; 16 chipped cache forms of glassy basalt ; antler implements ; carved bones and bone implements ; a carved piece of antler ; a celt of green stone ; 2 wedges of antler ; fragments of beaver-teeth ; copper clay ; bone awls ; a stone object. (See Figs. 336 *a*, 340 *b*, 345, 348.)

$\frac{16}{2690}-\frac{16}{2695}$. Charred human bones No. 3 (found 80 ft. south of No. 1 ; depth, about 6 inches) ; 10 chipped cache forms of glassy basalt ; a whetstone ; dentalium shells ; 3 flakes of glassy basalt ; 5 pendants made of the cores of claws. (See Figs. 331 *c*, 368.)

$\frac{16}{2696}-\frac{16}{2733}$. Charred human bones No. 4 (found 20 ft. south of No. 1 ; depth, about 3 inches) ; a perforated stone object ; a whetstone ; chipped forms of glassy basalt and other stone, including points, a scraper, and a drill ; 3 pieces of mica ; 9 pieces of fresh-water unio shells ; burned dentalium shells ; cylindrical shell beads ; oblong flat bone beads ; fragments of bone implements ; pieces of carved bone ; a burned pendant made of an elk-tooth ; burned pendants made of the cores of claws ; a tibia of a small mammal ; pieces of antler implements, some burned ; yellow material ; a bone pendant ; pieces of a burned antler handle for a root-digger ; barbed harpoon-points made of bone, and partly burned. (See Figs. 337 *b*, 352 *a*, *c*, 354 *a*, *c*, 370, 372 *b*, 381.)

GOVERNMENT HILL, NEAR KAMLOOPS.

$\frac{16}{2734}-\frac{16}{2772}, \frac{16}{5012}-\frac{16}{5014}$. Surface finds. (See Figs. 332 *b*, 338 *a*, 343, 347.)

$\frac{16}{2784}-\frac{16}{2803}$. Grave 1 (Plate XXVI), indicated on the surface by some scattering dentalium shells, and an oval (three feet long by two feet wide) of brown spots, at intervals of a few inches. These proved to be the ends of decayed fragments of a canoe made of Alaska cedar (*Chamæcyparis Nootkaensis*) daubed with red ochre. These pieces were standing on end around the body. Outside of this oval were the ends of four poles made of red cedar (*Thuya gigantea* Nutt.). They were set at regular intervals around the grave. The pieces of canoe extended down two feet and a half ; but as the wind shifts the surface sand, and since they were rotted down to the surface of the soil, it seems probable that they were originally much longer. The body may have been placed on the surface, the stakes and pieces of canoe forming a little burial-tent similar to the one found in the Nicola Valley. When the sand was blown into the tent, it preserved the lower portion, while the upper part was destroyed by natural forces. The body, probably that of a woman about twenty years of age, lay on its left side, with head towards the east, and legs slightly flexed, so that the thigh-bones were about at right angles to the vertebral column. It was wrapped in a fabric daubed with red ochre, and in pieces of skin. The whole bundle was bound with cords about a quarter of an inch in diameter, made of three strands of vegetable material twisted to the right. The fibres of each strand were twisted to the left. Four strings of dentalia, short cylindrical shell beads, and long cylindrical copper beads, arranged on a string, extended across the forehead. Similar copper beads, dentalia, and pendants made of teeth, some being the canine teeth of elk, others the incisor teeth of deer, were found at the neck. A bag about one foot long by three inches wide, made of fabric, extended from near the shoulders to the middle of the back. It contained beaver-tooth dice, bone needles, an iron awl in a bone handle, five bone tubes, chips of glassy basalt, a bone pendant, bearberry-seeds, and two bone objects showing traces of windings. Particles of red ochre permeated the bag and the surrounding soil. (See Figs. 357 d, 358 g, 367, 369, 371, 375 c.) The iron awl found in this grave is the only object showing contact with the whites, and iron secured by barter from the whites was not found in any of the other graves except in the long wooden boxes known to have been made since the arrival of the Hudson Bay Company's agents.

$\frac{16}{2804}-\frac{16}{2814}$. Grave (2 located 42 feet south of Grave 1).—Somewhat similar to Grave 1; but, instead of pieces of a canoe, poles had been placed around the body. They enclosed a space three feet in diameter. Their tops had been burned off about a foot below the surface or three feet above their lower ends. The skeleton, that of a woman about thirty years of age, was found two feet and a half deep, below the sand strata, resting on a hard gravel, which was exceedingly compact. The head was to the west, while the knees were flexed to the chest. The left hand was at the left shoulder, and the right arm was similarly flexed. Some bones of a small mammal were found near the right shoulder. A birch-bark dish rested over the thighs. The body was wrapped in a fabric of woven vegetable fibre. Outside of this was matting made of cat-tail stalks woven as shown in Fig. 131 c, Part IV. Pieces of wood, possibly parts of a bow or spear-handle, were found on the south side of the right arm bones. A chipped knife made of glassy basalt, which shows traces of gum along its base, was found crushed into one of these pieces of wood, and may have been hafted in it. A bone awl with traces of cord that had been wound around it was found at the right elbow on the south side of the grave. A little square piece of stone, fragments of bone, a beaver-tooth, a whetstone, and four chips were also found south of the right elbow (see Fig. 332 c). The exceedingly dry climate and good drainage of the hill would preserve wooden objects and fabrics for a very long period.

$\frac{16}{2773}-\frac{16}{2780}$. Cache 1 (depth in shifting sand, about 6 inches).—127 chipped flakes of glassy basalt; a scraper and point of the same material; 7 pebbles which may have been hammer-stones; a piece of slate; a whetstone; pieces of bone. (See Fig. 332 f.)

$\frac{16}{2781}, \frac{16}{2782}$ Cache 2 (depth, about 6 inches).—12 flakes of glassy basalt; 3 hammer-stone pebbles.

$\frac{16}{2610}-\frac{16}{2624}, \frac{16}{2826}-\frac{16}{2829}$. Surface finds near Kamloops. (See Figs. 336 b, 357 c.)

NICOLA VALLEY.

$\frac{16}{7042}, \frac{16}{7043}$. Surface finds.

$\frac{99}{2612}$. Grave 1 (6 miles up the valley).—The skeleton, which rested on the rock-slide material, was in a tent of poles about seven feet long, covered with mats made of common cat-tail stalks

(*Typha latifolia*) sewed together as shown in Fig. 131 *c*, Part IV. The talus material covered this to a depth of about two feet. The skull was south, the face east ; the body, which was that of an old woman, lay upon its back, with the legs closely flexed and projecting upward. There were no objects with the skeleton or in the tent.

$\frac{9\,9}{2\,6\,1\,3}, \frac{1\,6}{7\,0\,4\,4}-\frac{1\,6}{7\,0\,5\,1}.$ Grave 2 (also covered by about two feet of talus). — The skull was south, the face east, the body lying on its back with legs closely flexed and knees projecting upward. A broken nephrite celt, a rubbed stone, a fresh-water unio shell, 2 chipped pieces, 2 chipped points, and a chip of glassy basalt, were found at the right side (see Fig. 351 *c*). The leg-bones were much decomposed, and badly broken by the rocks.

MOUTH OF NICOLA LAKE.

$\frac{1\,6}{6\,9\,8\,4}.$ Surface find. — Skeletons of two children found near here were eighteen inches deep, massed in a pocket of black soil, which extended down into the yellow subsoil about six inches. The top of each grave, which was level with the surrounding surface, was covered with five or six bowlders.

$\frac{9\,9}{2\,6\,1\,1}, \frac{1\,6}{7\,0\,4\,1}, \frac{1\,6}{7\,0\,4\,4}.$ Skeleton of a man found near the children mentioned above was known to be that of a large person from Lytton, who was born at Cisco. He was murdered in the fifties, and his family buried him. The body lay upon the back, with head to the west, the legs closely flexed, and was covered with woven fabrics, some of which had evidently been secured from the whites. A bundle of half-round wooden rods about three feet long, with a longitudinal groove down the middle of the flat side, was found in the grave. The tibia and fibula had been broken; and the latter had fully healed, while the former was still in the process of healing. The tradition regarding this burial does not relate that the man was ever lame. The fact that the grave is of recent date proves that this style of burial prevailed until the middle of the century, and suggests that the children's graves, being similar to and near his, may also be recent. Graves of this type known to be very old have not been found by us in the Thompson River region.

HEAD OF NICOLA LAKE.

$\frac{1\,6}{7\,0\,4\,0}.$ Surface find.

$\frac{1\,6}{6\,9\,8\,6}-\frac{1\,6}{6\,9\,8\,8}.$ Found in excavating.

$\frac{9\,9}{2\,6\,0\,3}.$ Grave 1 (a child) in the talus on the Indian reserve here. — The head was towards the east, the face towards the north. The skeleton was covered with about four inches of earth and eighteen inches of rock-slide material. It rested upon its right side, and a thin stratum of yellow ochre was found in the earth near the head. This was probably the yellow paint from the face or garments. Among the rocks near this grave a piece of a human occiput was found, which bore knife-marks, as though the head had been cut off.

$\frac{9\,9}{2\,6\,0\,5}, \frac{1\,6}{6\,9\,8\,9}-\frac{1\,6}{6\,9\,9\,9}.$ Grave 2. — The bones, which were fully bleached, rested on the surface of the soil, and were covered to a depth of about two feet by the rock-slide material. The head was east, face west, and the legs were closely flexed. A double-edged celt of nephrite nearly fourteen inches in length was found lying diagonally across the chest, with its grooved edge southwest, curved corners northwest, and most perfectly formed edge to the southwest. A bone sap-scraper, beaver-teeth, two bone implements, and a piece of pointed wood, were found at the top of the skull. Dentalium shells and an awl of bone or antler were found under the head. Baptiste, the Indian guide, believed this to be a girl's head-scratcher. A knife of glassy basalt was found under the left upper arm, and a wooden cylinder at the left elbow. The skeleton of a dog, also fully bleached, was found with the head west, and tail near the left shoulder of the skeleton.

$\frac{99}{2606}, \frac{16}{7000}-\frac{16}{7010}.$ Grave 3.—The skeleton rested upon the soil, and was covered to a depth of one foot with rock. The body lay upon the back, with the head west, face east, and legs flexed, the knees projecting upward. The right hand was flexed to the shoulder. Three beaver-teeth and a celt of nephrite over thirteen inches in length, with grooved side down and blade west, were found on the right side of the skull. Near the blade of the celt was found a chipped point of glassy basalt daubed with red ochre. A drinking-tube lay near the top of the skull, and a small celt of nephrite was secured from under the head. A bone needle, such as was used for sewing tules into mats, and a finer bone needle, were found parallel to this celt, and with it a double-bladed celt somewhat larger in size, also made of nephrite, with grooved side down, the square blade east, and the diagonal blade west. Near the pelvis was a chip of glassy basalt. Pieces of burned skull-bones and a chipped point of chalcedony were also found in the grave. Probably the lodges of the victims were set on fire by the war-party, which may account for the charred appearance of the bones. (See Fig. 358 a, b.)

$\frac{99}{2607}, \frac{16}{7011}-\frac{16}{7018}.$ Grave 4.—The skull was found about one foot west of the skull of the third. The body lay upon the surface of the ground, and was covered with small fragments of rock of the talus. Above these were bowlders weighing from thirty to a hundred pounds. A post stood at the head, which was to the east, and faced northward. The right hand was flexed to the shoulder. Dentalium shells were found under the skull, and matting made of cat-tail stalks sewed together, as shown in Fig. 131 c, Part IV, was taken from under the back and arms. A handle made of antler, for a root-digger, lay along the left upper arm, with its larger end at the shoulder, where were also a little mass of red ochre, a beaver-tooth, beads made of sections of dentalium shells, a small arrow-point of glassy basalt with its point towards the head, and a bone needle. Under the middle of the back was found a cylinder of copper, copper beads, and short cylindrical beads of sections of dentalium shells. A bone of a bear, and a stray radius of an adult human being, were found in the rocks above the pelvis of this skeleton.

$\frac{16}{6685}, \frac{16}{7019}-\frac{16}{7038}.$ Grave 5.—The skeleton was that of a youth, and lay on the surface of the soil, under eighteen inches of rock-slide material. The head was south, with face west. The left parietal and some bones of the body were stained with copper salts, and covered with woven fabric and deer-skin on which the hair still remained. South of the head was a bundle, probably a pouch made of deer-skin from which the hair had not been removed. Four strands of beads made of sections of dentalium shells strung upon a cord were around the neck. The whole formed a necklace tied at the back. From the front a copper pendant was suspended. A copper object of similar shape was found with a mass of material around the skull. Being suspended by a string which passed through a whole dentalium shell and a bead, it seems probable that the whole formed an ear-pendant. Another copper ornament, and dentalium shells, probably the remains of the other ear-pendant, were found in the same mass. A piece of rope or slow-match of shredded cedar-bark, to which was attached a skin of a small mammal, part of a bird-skin, a perforated bear-claw through which was part of a thong, and two copper pendants, were found in this mass of material. A celt made of nephrite lay with its irregular blade east, flat side up, near the beads and skin. It may have been in the pouch. The skull of a dog was found among the rocks covering the skeleton, and with it was a large wedge made of antler. (See Figs. 349 b, 363, 365, 366.)

$\frac{16}{7033}-\frac{16}{7035}.$ Grave 6 contained only one bone, the fibula of an adult person. It rested on the surface of the soil, covered by rock-slide material. Three chipped pieces of stone, a natural piece of chalcedony of cone shape, and five fantastically chipped points of glassy basalt, were also in the grave. Among the stones above the grave was found a celt of green nephrite. (See Fig. 334, b–e.)

$\frac{99}{2608}.$ Grave 7.—The skeleton rested on the surface of the soil, under eighteen inches of rock-slide material. The skull was to the east, face west, and the legs were closely flexed. The hands covered the face.

$\frac{99}{2609}$, $\frac{16}{7036}$, $\frac{16}{7037}$. Grave 8.—The skeleton rested on the surface of the soil, below about eighteen inches of rock-slide material. The neck-bones were west, and there was no skull. The legs were flexed. The left arm as far as the elbow extended along the side, the fore-arm then crossed to the pelvis. An ornamented implement made of antler lay diagonally across the breast, with the point towards the left wrist, and the butt towards the right elbow. Two elk-tooth pendants were found near the neck. (See Figs. 360 *b*, 378.)

$\frac{99}{2610}$, $\frac{16}{7038}$, $\frac{16}{7039}$, $\frac{16}{7052}$, $\frac{16}{7053}$. Grave 9.—The skeleton rested on the surface of the soil, and was covered to a depth of about one foot by rock-slide material. Above the skeleton were found pieces of birch-bark, the bones of a dog colored with red ochre, a chipped point of glassy basalt, and pieces of charcoal. The body rested on its back, with the hands to the shoulders, and legs flexed in such a manner that the knees projected upward, the head turned towards the east. At the side, extending from the femur to the skull, were fragments of a much-decayed wooden bow. It was of very hard, close-grained wood, and was elliptical, tending towards lozenge-shape, in cross-section. The surface was very smooth, and one side was ornamented with little cuneiform incisions arranged like the marks on birch-bark. A celt of green nephrite, with the long grooved side down, and the square blade toward the feet, lay with the bow, and parallel to it. A shorter celt with one broken corner lay with this, having its square blade towards the feet. Its grooved side was down and bevelled side up. (See Fig. 349, *a*, *c*.)

APPENDIX II.

ADDITIONAL INFORMATION REGARDING SPECIMENS FIGURED IN PART III.

The following additional information regarding specimens figured in Part III of this volume was secured at Spences Bridge and in Nicola Valley during 1899, from Baptiste, an old Indian shaman living in the valley ; Michel, an intelligent old Indian of Lytton ; SalictE, chief at Nicola Lake ; and the brothers of the last named, James Michel Tcilaxitca and Charlie Tcilaxitca. When Baptiste and Michel were children, objects of white manufacture were rarely if ever seen by them.

Fig. 1. This Baptiste considered to represent an unfinished pipe. The theory seems plausible, although the pipe would have been very small. Michel of Lytton thought it represented a small hammer, to be hafted in a little handle and used by a slave or servant to crush food for a rich and toothless old person, the food being put between two pieces of skin or fabric, which accounts for the absence of a bruised surface on the object.

Fig. 20. Baptiste thought that this represented a beaver-spear, and that a string was tied through the perforation in the base, so that the point might not pull out of the handle and allow the animal to escape with it. This opinion was also held by Michel of Lytton.

Fig. 38. According to Baptiste, this represents an anvil upon which to crush food in mouthful quantities for rich, toothless old persons when travelling, larger anvils being used when in camp (see Part III, p. 139).

Fig. 39. This is thought by Baptiste to represent a stone that, when covered with skin, was used as a ball in the game described on p. 279 of Part IV. Mr. Teit approved this opinion, but Michel of Lytton believed it to have been covered with skin and used as a club-head (see Part IV, p. 264). It is hardly probable that specimens like the one shown in Fig. 247, which are not nearly so spherical even as the one illustrated in Fig. 39, should have been used in the game.

Fig. 49 illustrates a specimen which Baptiste and Mr. Teit agree was undoubtedly used for such purposes as chipping arrow-points, carving wood, and cutting out steatite pipes. They were not impressed with the opinion of Michel of Lytton, that it was used for cutting nephrite (see footnote, p. 416).

Fig. 50. Baptiste considered this to represent a large foreshaft and head for an arrow such as was formerly used to kill horses, dogs, and the like, to be placed on the grave of their owner. He later concluded that it represented a knife, but said that it resembled these arrow-heads.

Fig. 51. Michel of Lytton considered this to represent a knife for cutting soft inner bark when the sap runs in April (see Fig. 340 and Part IV, p. 233). Later Baptiste said that very brave bear-hunters formerly used such an implement to thrust down the bear's throat, placing one end against the roof of his mouth, and the other on his tongue when he opened his mouth. James Michel Tcilaxitca approved this opinion. Both said that Michel of Lytton was mistaken, but he was not seen after this.

Fig. 52. According to Baptiste, this represents a chisel used to scrape small pieces of skin.

Fig. 53. This, he considered, represents an awl.

Fig. 54. Baptiste also believed this to represent a scraper for small pieces of skin, and he stated that needles and small bone awls were laid in the natural groove and wrapped there to keep them from being broken when not in use.

Fig. 55. Mr. Teit thought this might represent a sap-cutter. Baptiste believed it to represent a flaker for making arrow-points. Michel of Lytton concurred in Baptiste's opinion (see Fig. 340).

Fig. 56. Michel of Lytton considered this to represent part of a trap used to catch ground-hogs as they issue from their burrows. He called it an i'xuap, and said they were made of wood, bone, or "horn." No other evidences of traps were found by us.

Fig. 59. Baptiste believed this to represent a spindle-whorl for spinning dog-hair and mountain-goat wool. Michel of Lytton agreed, and said that some of them were made of wood, and others of bone.

Fig. 65. Baptiste said that this, like Fig. 54, represented a case for awls and needles as well as a scraper.

Fig. 84. Charlie Tcilaxitca believed this to represent an ornament worn on the hair, behind the shoulders, by chiefs' daughters.

Fig. 87. Charlie Tcilaxitca thought ornaments of this kind were worn on the chest by daughters of chiefs (see p. 425).

Fig. 95. This was shown to Mr. Teit, Baptiste, Charlie Tcilaxitca, and also Michel of Lytton. All of them insisted that the object, which is figured as two-thirds natural size, is a sap-scraper such as was used when they were children. Such evidence, in addition to the similarity of the object to modern sap-scrapers, seems to satisfactorily prove that it was used for this purpose.

Figs. 96–98. Charlie Tcilaxitca says that such pendants were used for each ear, as well as in large numbers for necklaces (see p. 426).

Fig. 99. Charlie Tcilaxitca said of this, that when a child he saw nose-ornaments in use which were made of dentalium shells with a hair tassel at each end similar to the specimen shown in Fig. 99. Baptiste and Mr. Teit both approved this remark (see Fig. 197, Part IV), and also agreed that such shells with tassels may also have served as ear-pendants such as are described on p. 222, Part IV. Mr. Teit said that all the Indians know of the use of such nose-ornaments.

Fig. 102. Baptiste considers this to represent a drinking-tube; and Michel of Lytton confirmed the statement, saying that at the time of the ceremonies when young girls received their manitous, they were not allowed to use a cup, but had to drink through such a tube for the period of one year. Modern drinking-tubes are illustrated on p. 313 of Part IV.

Figs. 107, 109, 110. Baptiste said that these represented objects which were kept simply because they were considered nice or valuable.   Charlie Tcilaxitca had the same opinion regarding Figs. 109 and 110.

Fig. 114 was submitted to Mr. Teit, Chief Salicte, Charlie Tcilaxitca, and Baptiste.   They all agree that it is a fixture for a dog-halter to keep the loop from slipping up and choking the dog ; also that the carving represents the manitou of the owner of the dog, and was first seen in a dream. It resembles, in general shape, and in having a mouth and tail, the specimens known to be such fixtures (see Part IV, p. 245).

Fig. 116.   Mr. Teit said that this represented a piece of copper that was probably being rolled around the cylindrical stick to form it into a long bead, and that, as the person was at work upon it immediately before death, it was buried with him.

PLATE XXIV.

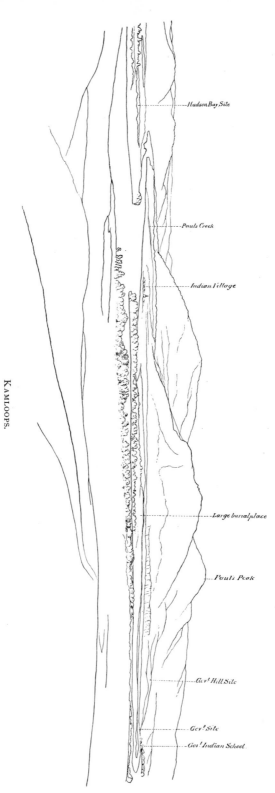

KAMLOOPS.
(Explanation of Plate XXIV.)

Hudson Bay Site

Pauls Creek

Indian Village

Large burial place

Pauls Peak

Gov.^t Hill Site

Gov.^t Site

Gov.^t Indian School

Plate XXIV.

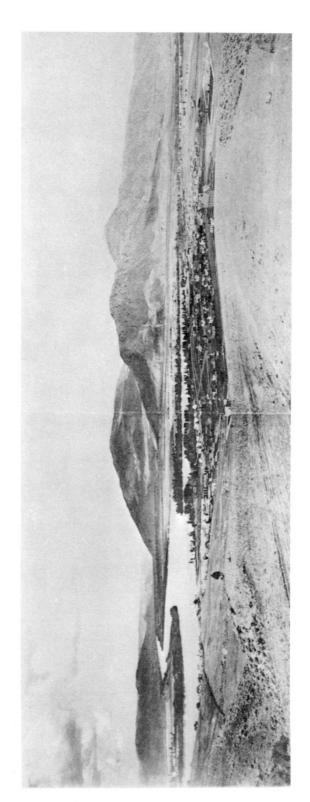

KAMLOOPS.

Archæology of the Thompson River Region.

FIG. 1.   ROCK-SLIDE, WITH GRAVES, NICOLA VALLEY.

FIG. 2.   ROCK-SLIDE, WITH GRAVES, EAST END OF NICOLA LAKE.

Archæology of the Thompson River Region.

FIG. 1.   VIEW OF GRAVE ON GOVERNMENT HILL, KAMLOOPS.

FIG. 2.   VIEW OF THE SAME GRAVE, OPEN.

Archæology of the Thompson River Region.

ERRATA.

Page 152, in legend to Fig. 95, " $\frac{1}{3}$ nat. size " should read " $\frac{2}{3}$ nat. size."

Page 183, 2d line of footnote, " Fig. 122 " should read " Fig. 120."

Page 223, in legend to Fig. 198, " $\frac{65}{4512}$ " should read " $\frac{16}{4512}$."

" Pages 391, 392," Part IV, Appendix, should read " pages 390A, 390B."